ARCHITECTURAL DESIGN

EDITORIAL OFFICES:
42 LEINSTER GARDENS, LONDON W2 3AN
TEL: + 44 71 402 2141 FAX: + 44 171 723 9540

EDITOR: Maggie Toy
EDITORIAL TEAM: Ellie Duffy, Ramona
Khambatta, Jane Richards
DESIGNER: Alex Young

CONSULTANTS: Catherine Cooke, Terry Farrell,
Kenneth Frampton, Charles Jencks, Heinrich Klotz,
Leon Krier, Robert Maxwell, Demetri Porphyrios,
Kenneth Powell, Colin Rowe, Derek Walker

SUBSCRIPTION OFFICES:
UK: ACADEMY GROUP LTD
42 LEINSTER GARDENS
LONDON W2 3AN
TEL: + 44 171 402 2141 FAX: + 44 171 723 9540

USA AND CANADA:
JOHN WILEY & SONS, INC
JOURNALS ADMINISTRATION DEPARTMENT
695 THIRD AVENUE
NEW YORK, NY 10158
TEL: + 1 212 850 6645 FAX: + 1 212 850 6021
CABLE JONWILE TELEX: 12-7063
E-MAIL: subinfo@jwiley.com

ALL OTHER COUNTRIES:
VCH VERLAGSGESELLSCHAFT MBH
BOSCHSTRASSE 12, POSTFACH 101161
69451 WEINHEIM
FEDERAL REPUBLIC OF GERMANY
TEL: + 49 6201 606 148 FAX: + 49 6201 606 184

Subscription rates for 1997 (incl p&p): *Annual subscription price*: UK only £74.00, World DM 195 for regular subscribers. *Student rate*: UK only £53.00, World DM 156 incl postage and handling charges. *Individual issues*: £18.95/DM 45.00 (plus £2.30/DM 5 for p&p, per issue ordered).
For the USA and Canada: *Architectural Design* is published six times per year (Jan/Feb; Mar/Apr; May/Jun; Jul/Aug; Sept/Oct; and Nov/Dec) by Academy Group Ltd, 42 Leinster Gardens, London W2 3AN, England and distributed by John Wiley & Son, Inc, Journals Administration Department, 695 Third Avenue, New York, NY 10158, USA. Annual subscription price; US $142.00 including postage and handling charges; special student rates available at $105.00, single issue $29.95. Periodicals postage paid at Jamaica, NY 11431. Air freight and mailing in the USA by Publications Expediting Services Inc, 200 Meacham Ave, Elmont, NY 11003: Send address changes to: 'title', c/o Publications Expediting Services Inc, 200 Meacham Ave, Elmont, NY 11003. Printed in Italy. All prices are subject to change without notice. [ISSN: 0003-8504]

CONTENTS

ARCHITECTURAL DESIGN **MAGAZINE**

Peter Greenaway *interview with Bridget Elliott and* *Anthony Purdy* • **Simon Ungers** • **Tomasz Samek** • **Tadashi Kawamata** • *Academy Highlights*

Simon Ungers, *Topos*, 1995

ARCHITECTURAL DESIGN **PROFILE** No 128

FRONTIERS: ARTISTS & ARCHITECTS

Robert Maxwell • *Clare Melhuish* • **Neil Spiller** • *Michael Spens* • **Will Alsop** • *James Carpenter* • **MacCormac Jamieson Prichard** • *OM Ungers and Ian Hamilton Finlay* • **Ian Ritchie** • *Pawson Williams Architects* • **Future Systems** • *John Lyall Architects* • **Bauman Lyons Architects** • *Cezary M Bednarski + Peter Fink* • **James Turrell** • *Jane Harrison and David Turnbull* • **Sauerbruch Hutton Architects** • *Richard Wentworth* • **Pierre d'Avoine with Heather Ackroyd and Dan Harvey** • *Richard Wilson* • **Tania Kovats in collaboration with Levitt Bernstein Associates**

Richard Wilson, Baltic Flour Mills project, 1996

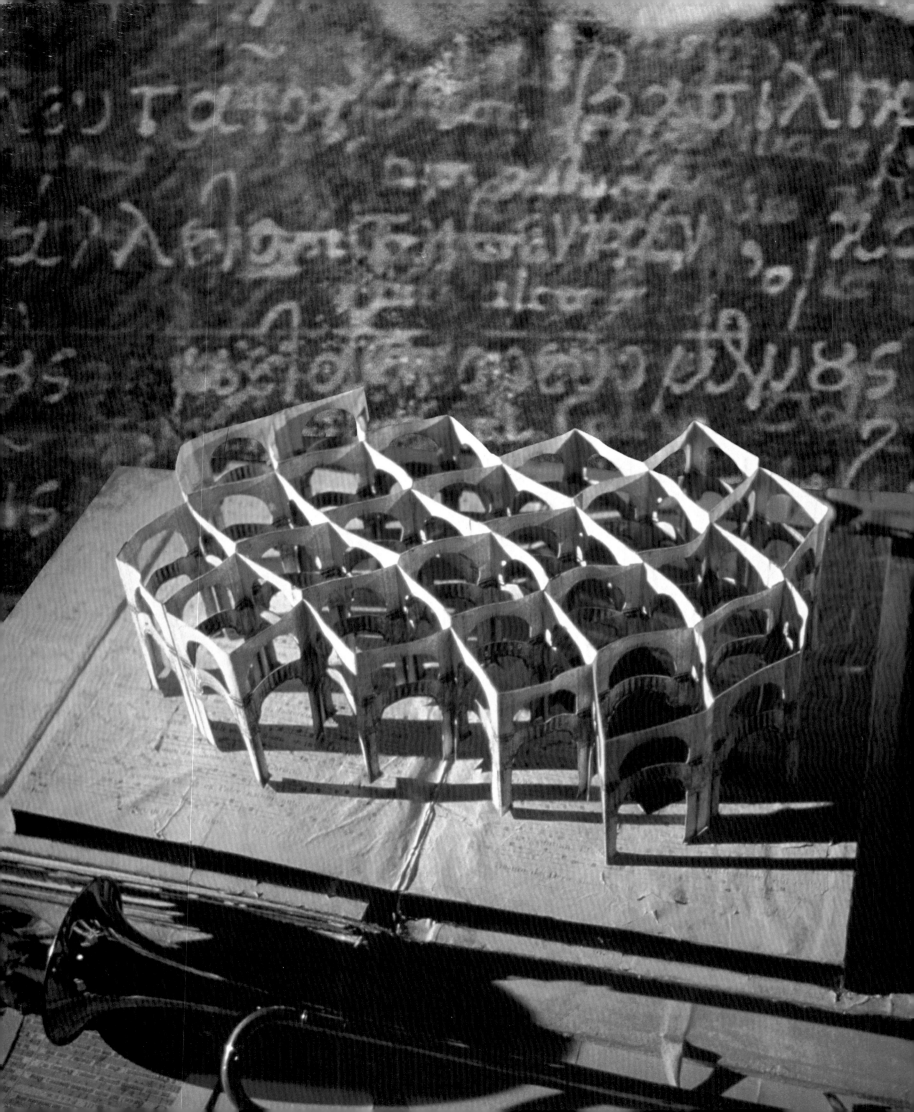

AN INTERVIEW WITH PETER GREENAWAY

Bridget Elliott and Anthony Purdy

Peter Greenaway received us at The VUE, tucked away behind a red door at the end of an alley in Hammersmith, London, on the afternoon of October 7, 1996. After a general chat, he offered the observation that, since our book was already finished, the interview might seem rather like a post mortem. For a variety of reasons, not least of which is the difficulty of sustaining 'death of the author' theories when faced with a very lively Greenaway, we prefer to think of it as a post scriptum. Reproduced here are a number of reflections drawn from a longer conversation. Our thanks to Peter Greenaway for a very pleasant afternoon, to Eliza Poklewski Koziell for her warm welcome at The VUE, and to Zoë Purdy for her help in transcribing the tapes.

You must be a pretty avid museum goer?

But not necessarily academic museums. If you regard a cathedral as a museum, or if you regard a zoo as a museum, I would certainly try to make a visit to these sorts of collections as well as to the other more orthodox institutions.

What do you look for when you go to a museum?

Principles of collection, principles of collation, the way things are organised. I would look for presentation as well as individual objects, because the medium in which the objects and ideas are organised, and also its history and its background is significant for the way in which you appreciate the objects within it. There's a general feeling that museums are supposed to be neutral places. I don't think any museum in the world can be that, though it often strives so hard to be. Certainly in my curatorial activity, I might go to the opposite end, and say, 'Look, this is a very subjective view of a particular situation, number of objects, ideas . . .' We should include the architects and the designers of the museum or gallery building too – the architect is important in shaping how collections are perceived and organised. The siting of the museum café could be more important than any other single architectural decision.

Do you find yourself part of a community in terms of the new museology any more than you would in terms of your cinema?

I'm English, and I suppose that, apart from the Pre-Raphaelites who met perhaps for six weeks and then never again, I cannot think of a coterie of English creative people who have ever stayed together as a community or club – whether painters, writers or museologists. Maybe we could not say that of the French – Impressionists, Nabis, Fauves, nouvelle vague – nor possibly of the Germans, nor maybe of the Italians, but the English always insist on remaining isolated individuals.

Do you ever feel like an exhibition piece yourself or are you fairly philosophical about all the attention?

I have always felt my job as a filmmaker should extend after the projector had shut down. Since I hope I pursue a cinema of ideas, and the ideas are always more interesting than the films, I want to continue to talk about the ideas, so in that sense I'm all

for the exposure. But sometimes I would agree that the artist really ought to go into total hibernation and not show his face. But then the opposite point of view can be canvassed. Certainly film-distributors ask to see the face behind the work, and ask to bring that face forward to meet the professionals, if not the audience. But there's still a way in which I've sometimes wondered whether the author is necessarily the best person to talk to about his or her work. I can remember occasions when talking about a film, I have irredeemably antagonised a sympathetic viewer. In England, I have, in some quarters, been judged as elitist, bombastic, a cultural exhibitionist with a reputation for being mannerist and eclectic and confrontationalist and other pejorative things in my own public defence. Certainly 'too clever for his own good'. We are an old democracy: 'don't shove your head above the parapet, you'll get it knocked off'. Foreign audiences seem to be more intrigued than audiences at home. Certainly the audience abroad is much larger than the audience at home. I'm a marginal UK figure. Perhaps if I could start again, I should be a filmmaker without a face and without an extra-film voice. Because of some of the subject-matter and imagery in my films, I have noticed, when I walk through the arrivals hall in a foreign airport, the meeting-party expect a Sadean, cadaverous figure – a man who perhaps carries a coffin and rotting body parts in his luggage. When they see the orthodox English bourgeois, with all the usual associations, faces fall.

Where is *The Stairs* project right now? Is Barcelona going ahead?

There's been a Spanish election and a change of government, and a rearrangement of previously powerful people; art funding can depend, as Christo discovered, on who's in power, if only because the new boys need to be seen to be in disagreement with the old guard. So plans have changed and we will be making an exhibition in Barcelona called *Flying Over Water*, on the subject of the Icarus myth – not Icarus alone, but with an eye on all flying pioneers from Montgolfier, the Wright Brothers, Bleriot, Amy Johnson to Gagarin. Plans were very seriously discussed to stage the next exhibition of *The Stairs* in association with the Lisbon Trade Expo '98, and to consider at the same time, an exhibition on the Lisbon Earthquake. One of the most exciting characteristics for me about the staging of city-wide exhibitions, that I suppose Christo must have learnt many years ago, is that it's a grand, public exercise in social persuasion. And this can be more important indeed, than any aesthetic preoccupations. I've just returned from Israel, where there is enthusiasm for placing an exhibition of *The Stairs* in Jerusalem, an exhibition about touch and feel and body sensation of height, vertigo and gravity. We discussed the possibility of erecting one hundred tall towers all over the city. But the territorial, political and religious problems are formidable, to say the least. Every yard of turf is foreign territory to someone with a very strong vested interest indeed. Perhaps this very difficulty is the reason to do it.

You have a very obvious interest in architecture. It functions, for example, as a master metaphor in *Belly*. But there's relatively little contemporary architecture foregrounded in your films. Is there a reason for that?

Well, you've just seen *The Pillow Book*. Renzo Piano's airport at Kansai is featured, very noisily, and he prided himself on it being a very quiet airport. Pei's Hong Kong Bank and Foster's Hongkong and Shanghai Bank are in the background of some very early shots in the film. I suppose the creation, which was a collaboration with the design team, of that yacht-like building in *Drowning By Numbers* might be of interest as a forefronted modern building. We sent the plans on request to a Belgian builder. There isn't much opportunity or scope to use modern architecture in 17th-century films that feature the baroque. These movies had also become – deliberately – more and more interior and claustrophobic, more and more designed as an artifice in a studio. So I suppose the last time we were out and about in the known, visible world would have been with *Drowning By Numbers*. There are certainly various parts of *The Pillow Book* where we are out and about again. Talking about the next project – *The Tulse Luper Suitcase* – we intend to revisit favourite architectural sites around the world, and some of those indeed will be modern buildings.

It's interesting that the last three films before *The Pillow Book* were very much interior films and that, at the same time, in terms of your curatorial work, you were going out into the city. Is there some sort of symbiotic relationship between the two activities?

You make it sound a little manipulative, as though I was planning it that way, which I cannot claim is the case. It is refreshing to leave the artifices of the studio, and investigate real architectural spaces. And I have been aware that these possible mixtures of opposites have had other influences. As the result of increased figuration, increased crowd scenes in the movies, it's true that the paintings have become more and more reductive of figuration. They have always featured maps, diagrams and charts and lists. These characteristics have increased. There maybe is another factor which, I suppose, has more to do with the film's financial position – the notion of making the films in what we could call an A/B fashion. An A film, which is a little more popular and commercial, followed by a B film which is more experimental. *The Draughtsman's Contract* and *A Zed & Two Noughts* are examples. If we continue A/B, A/B, A/B, maybe we will stay alive creatively and financially. But we had two B pictures together – *Prospero's Books* and *The Baby of Mâcon*. And so it has become necessary to make an A picture again. We feel now – and this has become very self-conscious, whereas before it never was – that maybe *The Pillow Book* will be an A picture, which may open the doors to all those people who have been thinking that we were engaged in solely manufacturing claustrophobic interior studio-bound films.

If I may say something again on the question of my fascination with architecture . . . I gave a lecture recently to the Architectural Association in London about my formal or professional connections with architecture – that had to demonstrate such a background was entirely bogus. I have no training as an architect, though I have been asked to judge architectural competitions, including a recent Estonian architectural competition for an expensive post-office complex.

You had Nigel Coates on the set of *The Draughtsman's Contract*. What was he doing there?

I wanted somebody else – since my obligation was to direct the film and worry about the committal of script to celluloid – to do the drawings, and we asked him; but his drawings turned out to be inappropriate and, in the end, I made them myself. I always believe it has to be the communicator's fault and not the communicatee's, so it must be my problem. But the need for veracity is part of the essence of that film. The Draughtsman has a fetish to put down exactly what he sees. So it's a film about 'I draw what I see, not what I know'. And Nigel drew what he knew, not what he saw.

Amongst working architects, contemporary architects, which ones do you like?

Forgive the patriotism, but I support the English. I prefer Rogers to Foster, though I don't know what that tells you. Farrell I've always enjoyed. Despite the complaints about his two buildings on the Thames, I enjoy their strong symmetry and use of site. Also, Nouvel and much new French architecture, and I'm very interested in architects from the Middle and Far East. My enthusiasms are eclectic. The Portland Building was the first project I had come across and understood as bringing a postmodern metaphor into architecture. And I think that Graves, in some senses, was the hidden model for Stourley Kracklite in *The Belly of an Architect*, though he could claim no compliment for that, considering Kracklite built only six-and-a-half buildings.

Any interest in the deconstructionists?

My background and interest is classical, with the stream of verticals and horizontals as master-plan, with the grid as a dominant 20th-century painting proposition in the centre of the frame. My sympathies – sentimentally, nostalgically, intellectually and emotionally – would always go towards the notion of the classical form, the Apollonian universe, the continuing tradition in painting of della Francesca, Poussin, Mondrian, Jasper Johns and Sol le Wit.

There's a lot of talk about the public responsibility of the architect, but what about the public responsibility of the filmmaker? Or of the curator of an exhibition?

With painting and filmmaking I think its legitimate now, come sink or swim, to be governed and regulated by personal desire and taste, that a sense of responsibility must be my own seriousness of intent. I cannot think that Bacon and Picasso painted for anyone but themselves. It's still regarded as an act of arrogance to admit, as a filmmaker, that I must make films for myself. For me, it is arrogant to imagine I could make films for anyone else, especially since every member of the audience will want something different, and I am not privy to what that desire could be. Architecture still patently services individuals and communities in a way that painting, and, I would argue, film, does not. You cannot hide architecture – it's for common consumption – present and future. Historically, art-cultural activity outside architecture can exist without wholesale public consumption. It is, I suppose, possible, though difficult, to avoid painting, literature and music. Anything to do with the Hollywood presumption that films should be manufactured by committees for recognisable audiences, I would react against strongly. We suspect their responsibility is predicated by financial return, not moral or aesthetic consideration. Committee art is invariably bad. It is difficult to satisfactorily think of a situation where committee art did not make bad art.

How do you respond to those charges of elitism when they come?

The major traditions of the six traditional art-forms in the West have always been elitist. The study and practice of art has demanded education, specialist concentration and moneyed patronage; these things do not come easy or for free or without study. Cultural History repeatedly demonstrates that cultural artefacts that are valued are made for an elitist client or community or audience, whose interests are catered for by the collusion – in an elitist programme – of the creator.

But appreciating the object doesn't necessarily mean embracing the kind of elitist structures that produced it.

Not at all. But perhaps we should not baulk at the word 'elitism'. Conceivably everyone is elitist in some occupation or interest. It's like that unfortunate use of the word 'mannerist' which was so inappropriately attached to a certain period of very exciting work between the Renaissance and the Baroque and which has taken people down the wrong path because of the pejorative connotations of that particular adjective.

One thing that struck us in relation to _Prospero's Books_, but one could talk about it in relation to _The Pillow Book_ as well, was the idea that here you are with a brand new medium, exploring a new technology, and the content you choose to foreground is an old technology, which is something right out of McLuhan. Is that an interesting paradox for you, the idea that in a sense the new technologies allow you to become more artisanal in cinema than you could have been previously?

Well, I would disagree strongly with any modernist notion that there has to be a dramatic break from a historical continuity. It's self-evident that we are nothing without memory; though I acknowledge that history is subjective. A general metaphor for the next film is that there is no such thing as history, there are only historians. I read a great deal of history, and I enjoy sequence, chronology and continuity for their own sakes. I am dismayed that my own children will not be absolutely certain whether Henry VIII comes before Elizabeth or afterwards. People aren't even supposed to be interested in chronology anymore. It strikes me that if you don't have a chronology, how can you make use of all the other information? So the new technology should not be the broom that necessarily sweeps away the old – it can help understand the old better. A new language is used in _The Pillow-Book_ to discuss an old language – 3,000 years of Oriental calligraphy seen through the vocabulary of what some have described as a television language. This can perhaps be exemplified as an anxiety. All the world's texts have been self-evidently made by the body, with the particular relationship of the head to the arm to the hand to the pen to the paper. With ubiquitous contemporary keyboards we have broken the body-text link that started to decay with the printing-press, and accelerated with the typewriter. Is this just nostalgia? Is this just a reactionary notion? I don't think it is. One of the things I would forefront in all my films is the notion that we must stay very aware of our own physicality. As a filmmaker I am removed from it. Everything is happening through a prism at a distance, projected at a distance, and now with television and all its techniques – where touch and smell are entirely defunct we are down to three senses – how many senses can you lose and still function?

In _The Pillow Book_, if the body makes the text, then the best place for the text is back on the body. The abstracted texts of the West have removed themselves infinitely from the image meaning of this oriental potential but Oriental ideograms still acknowledge the idea that the history of Japanese literature was also the history of Japanese painting. They are bound together, but here, if you are a painter, you are not supposed to be a writer. If you are a writer, you are not supposed to be able to wield a brush. You'd imagine cinema to be the ideal place to marry these two opposites together, yet it hasn't seemed to have happened. In cinema images are enslaved to the text. So the notion of picking up the ideogram, the hieroglyph, the Oriental character as a possible template for cinema could be an interesting idea.

What about the question of the local? Are you optimistic about the kinds of globalism we're seeing now? Your own practice is becoming much more global in the sense that _The Pillow Book_, for example, has very different subjects and concerns from those of, say, _The Draughtsman's Contract_, which is partly about a successful practice that takes you to all these places and offers you new technologies that are not available to those people who are stuck at the local. In that sense you are privileged. But under the veneer of the universalism of the global village, are we actually losing the idea of the local?

Maybe we are. I am not so sure whether this is good or bad. English filmic traditions seem to me to be tedious in their localness. But seeking globalness can lead to blandness and banality because of the little and insufficient knowledge of the particular. To the irritation of many distributors, a lot of the Japanese and Oriental languages in the film are not translated – this might be cavalier – but I'm quite sure that in three decades time, kids in Toronto and Chicago will never hear a foreign language, which is obviously disastrous to their placement in the world and to the demise of cultural ideas. English thrives mightily because of its adaption and appropriation of other languages. With _The Pillow Book_, I wanted foreign audiences just to listen – there wasn't much chance of them understanding the meanings of the text but that doesn't mean it should be summarily smothered. People don't seem to even want to listen anymore to the sheer cadences and rhythms of these strange-sounding, foreign languages which are so beautiful and so fascinating. Global and local, home and abroad. I don't know how to answer this question with any absolute conviction, but I don't want to be particularly associated with English filmmaking that seems now to be investigating the minutiae of working-class opinion, attitude, habits, prejudices, in the way the middle classes were scrutinised earlier in the century. Seeking other areas, what do I give up? Do I give up my Englishness? My movies are very English. My camera team has often been French. My design team used to be Dutch. We do really feel as though we are good Europeans on a European enterprise. I'm Welsh by origin and the Welsh, with their minority language, are much better Europeans than the English anyway. But this is a problem, remembering the David Puttnam movie-credo, where we were supposed to be Anglo-American, producing films for the most part that were banal, never as good as what the Americans could do, and somehow bowdlerising or pastiching English culture for tourist appeal. So I don't really have an answer to your question. I will continue to push where I want to push and I will just have to suffer the consequences. Our next movie starts in the Utah desert looking for lost Mormon townships and ends up looking for Coleridge's Kubla Khan in Manchuria. Is that local?

An extract from Peter Greenaway: Architecture and Allegory _by Bridget Elliott and Anthony Purdy, Academy Editions, June 1997_

V

SIMON UNGERS
VARIOUS PROJECTS

Simon Ungers, an artist and architect who lives and works in New York and Cologne, was born in Germany in 1957. He studied architecture at Cornell University, Ithaca, New York, and was the founding partner of the architectural office UKZ Inc, in Ithaca.

As an architect, he and his partner Tom Kinslow received accolades for their T-House in Wilton, New York, in which an elevated rectangular library was cantilevered transversely across its residential base. As an artist, he has become known for his 'site constructions',

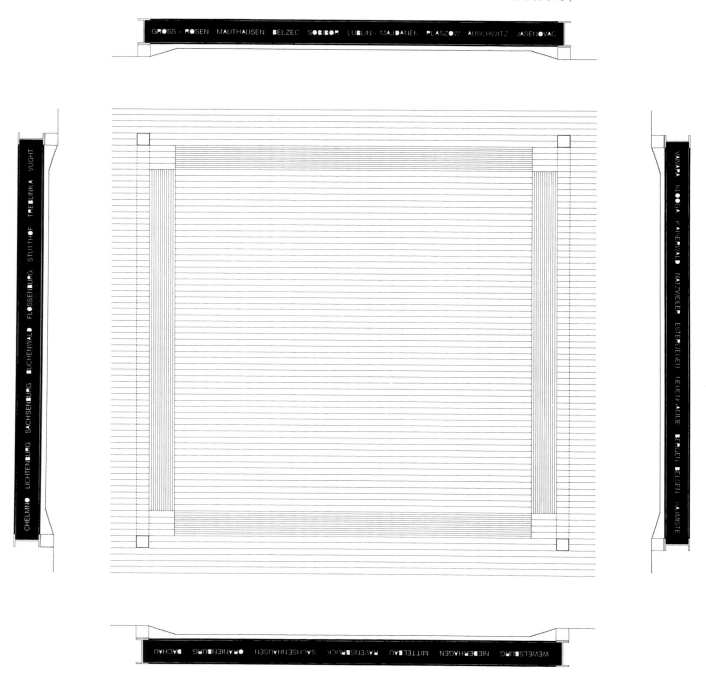

Berlin Holocaust Memorial Competition, 1994, joint winner

site-specific installations of large-scale minimalist objects. A striking example of this is *Red Slab in Space* (1993) where a horizontal, monolithic construction incorporates two pre-existing gallery columns into its own structure.

Ungers' work reflects ideas disseminated throughout Modernism, from early Russian Constructivism to the abstract Sublime as defined by Clement Greenberg via Kant and Burke to the Postmodernism of Jean-Francois Lyotard.

Topos, *Urban Structures, Kulturreferat Munich, 1995*

ABOVE: T-House, *Wilton, NY; OPPOSITE:* Red Slab in Space, *1993, Galerie Sophia Ungers, Cologne*

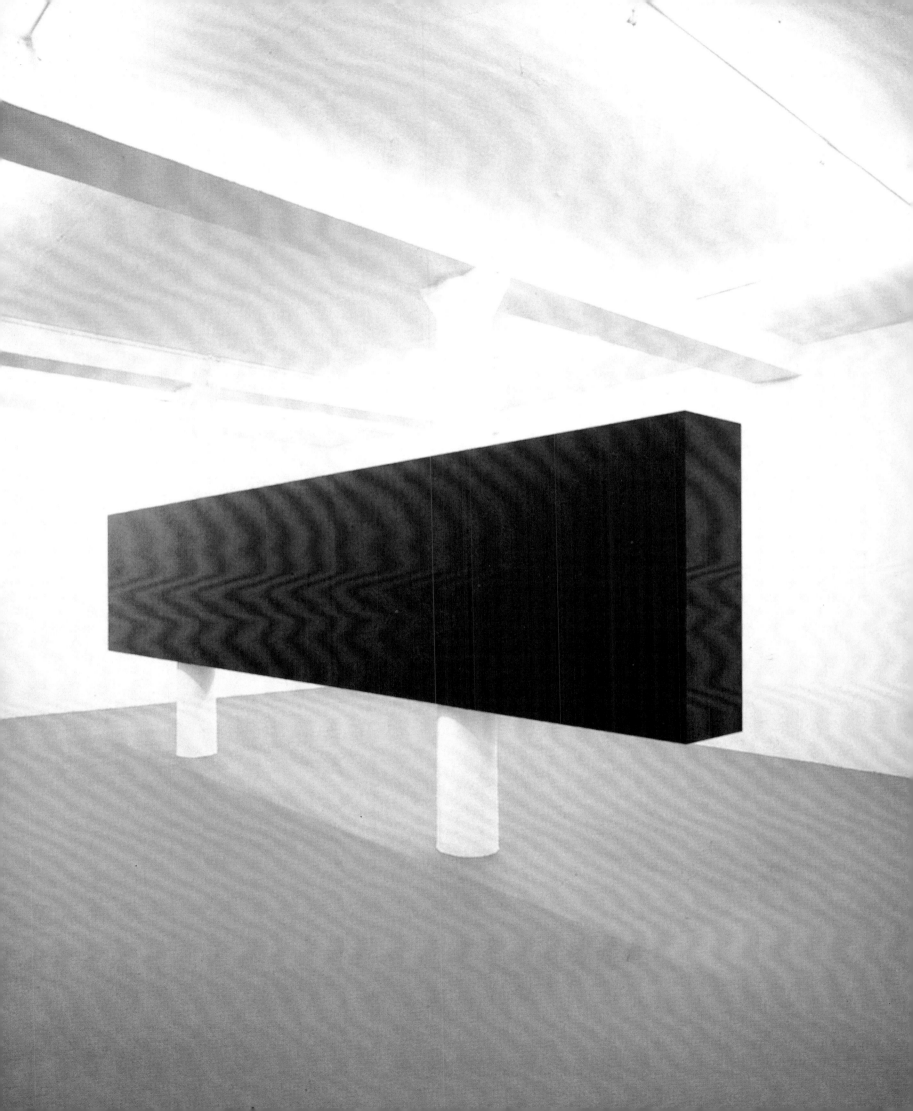

LEFT, FROM ABOVE: Intensity, 1994, New York; Asperity, 1994 – both at the Sandra Gering Gallery, New York; BELOW: Forum Chemnitz, 1995, Chemnitz, Germany

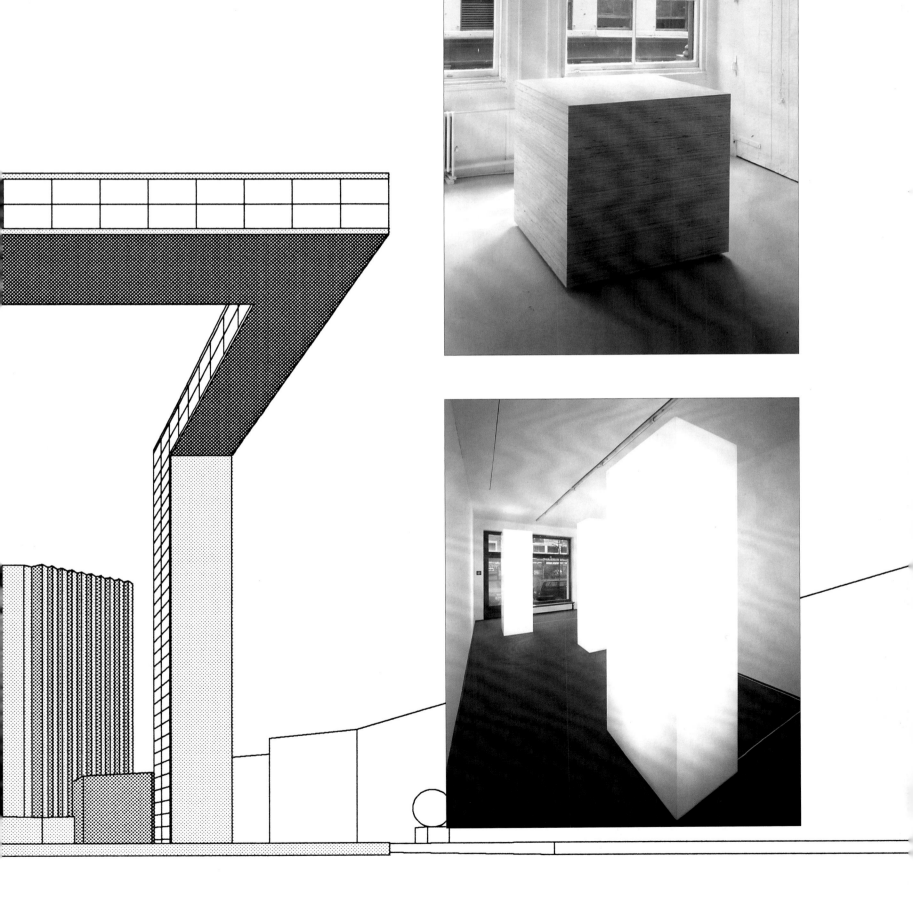

RIGHT, FROM ABOVE: Density, *1994, Sandra Gering Gallery, New York;* Three Monoliths, *1996, Galerie Sophia Ungers, Cologne*

TOMASZ SAMEK

WALLS
Münster Stadtmuseum

The Polish photographer Tomasz Samek (b. 1957) has lived in Münster, Germany, since 1982, where he has made interior surfaces of museums built in Germany in the 1980s and 90s – rather than the works of art they display – the subject of his work. He is particularly fascinated by the blank white exhibition walls of Postmodern 'temples of art' and has used tungsten film to photograph the play of natural and artificial light upon them – film highly sensitive to the colour spectrum and capable of capturing colours of light otherwise invisible to the human eye. This play of light and colour appears as a series of blue tones in the photographs, while the glow of neon lights appears green. The effect is that the surfaces themselves 'disappear' in these images, with only the light upon them being visible. The artworks on display in these museums are ignored as subjects, while the planes on which they hang are celebrated. The exhibition is a counterpoint to the underlying concept behind 'Sculpture Project 1997'.

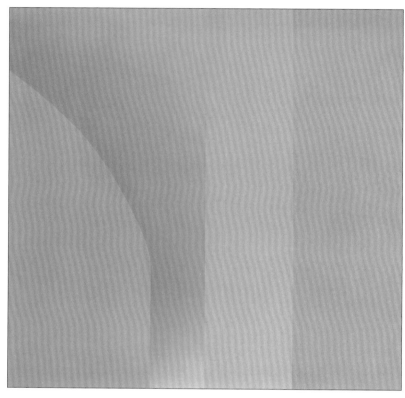

An exhibition of 30 large photographs of German museum walls, produced by Samek from 1993-97, is on show at the Stadtmuseum, Münster from 6 July-21 September 1997. Further details telephone: 0049 251 492 4502/03.

TADASHI KAWAMATA
DEMOLITION SCULPTURE
Serpentine Gallery

During its year-long renovation, the Serpentine Gallery is exhibiting five major sculptural commissions on the lawn outside the building. In contrast to the quiet setting of the Gallery's interior, this place for art is open and noisy, impinged upon by the construction site as well as subject to seasonal changes. Each project will constitute a lens through which the continuing transformation of the Serpentine can be seen.

Tadashi Kawamata's project, the final commission in the 'Serpentine: Inside Out' programme, will consist of materials retrieved from the demolition of the gallery building prior to its renovation. Using internal and external doors, windows and staircases he will create a structural framework on the gallery's lawn which reflects the Serpentine's architecture. Kawamata is well known for his monumental work, generally made from wood, which encroaches upon, and infiltrates, existing architecture. The opportunity to observe the development of the installation from its earliest stages will invite visitors to consider the relationship between the artwork and the changing face of a cherished landmark.

The Kawamata exhibition will run at the Serpentine Gallery, London, from 1 July-7 September 1997. Further information telephone: 0171 723 9072

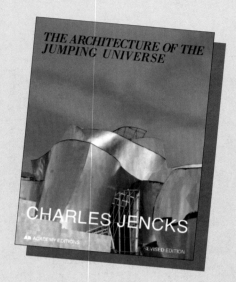

New Edition
THE ARCHITECTURE OF THE JUMPING UNIVERSE

A Polemic: How Complexity Science is Changing Architecture and Culture

Charles Jencks

- Updates the successful first edition of this widely acclaimed bestseller

- Presents a new theory of architecture

This inspired synthesis of art, design, science and philosophy charts a bold new course . . . Riveting.
    Paul Davies, author of *The Cosmic Blueprint*

This revised and enlarged new edition of Charles Jencks's bestseller brings the reader up to date with the progress of many of the projects that were in their infancy in this highly successful polemic, and also includes a number of new projects by some of today's most prominent architects. In addition to featuring works by figures like Peter Eisenman, Frank Gehry, Daniel Libeskind, Jeff Kipnis, Zvi Hecker and Greg Lynn, there are also detailed appraisals of various projects in Yokohama and the Storey Hall development in Melbourne, Australia. Curiously, Jencks also manages to include features on the Stealth Bomber aircraft and furniture design.

This new edition reveals Jencks's continued investigation and newly evolved conclusion of Chaos Theory and Complexity Science.

Paperback 1 85490 486 8
252 x 190 mm, 176 pages
Illustrated throughout, mainly in colour
£14.95 $25.00   DM30.00
Publication date: May 1997

FTL ARCHITECTS
Innovations in Tensile Structures
Architectural Monographs No. 48

- Features projects from this pioneering firm – world leaders in the field of tensile structures

- Increasingly popular method of building

- Technical details included

With over 800 projects and 30 awards for their designs, Future Tents Limited (or FTL as they are now popularly known) are acknowledged as pioneers in technological innovation. Todd Dalland and Nicholas Goldsmith, partners in FTL, attract clients who require lightweight membrane structures or deployable shelters, as well as those who understand the favourable economics of building with tensile technology.

Their evolution from the design fringe to the mainstream is a story of persistence, dedication, vision and a strong belief in themselves. Their unparalleled mastery of the tensile structure dates back to their student days at Cornell University 25 years ago, and Goldsmith's subsequent apprenticeship with Frei Otto – the world's leading expert in free-form tensile structures. Today, their commissions include roofs for sports stadia, entertainment complexes and circus pavilions, recreational facilities, and special on-site facilities for the military, in addition to more traditional (although highly unconventional) office and showroom design work for clients such as the DKNY clothing chain.

This monograph examines their *modus operandi*, their constant search for new materials that will enable them to design even more advanced structures, and looks at a number of their recent projects.

Paperback 1 85490 456 6
305 x 252 mm, 128 pages
Illustrated throughout, mainly in colour
£21.95 $38.00   DM57.00
Publication date: June 1997

TOKYO
World Cities

Edited by Botond Bognar

- An all encompassing view of Tokyo – one of the world's most exciting and vibrant cities

- Includes a glimpse of the city as it was, as it is today, as it might have been and as it may become in the future

As with the three previous volumes in this series, this is a large, lavishly illustrated book, documenting the historical development and future prospects for one of the world's most distinctive cities – Tokyo, the epitome of the Japanese city. It is an attempt to capture and reflect Tokyo's kaleidoscopic, heterogeneous and multi-focal disposition, wherein vistas overlap, boundaries are blurred, and any urban order that may exist is deeply buried and profoundly hidden.

In exploring Tokyo, Botond Bognar looks not only at the city itself but also at the outlying districts of Kawasaki, Yokohama and Makuhari, the suburban communities of Tama and Fujisawa, and the exciting waterfront developments and landfill projects in Tokyo Bay. Amongst the dozens of architects featured are many world-renowned Japanese architects such as Tadao Ando, Toyo Ito, Kisho Kurokawa, Arata Isozaki and Shin Takamatsu, plus the foreigners whose designs grace the city's skyline – Peter Eisenman, Sir Norman Foster, Cesar Pelli, Sir Richard Rogers and Aldo Rossi.

Contents include: Introduction – Tokyo as an Oriental City; The Past – From Edo to Tokyo; Unbuilt Visions – Tokyo as It Could Have Been; The Present – Tokyo as It Is; The Future – Tokyo as It Will Be in the 21st century; Tokyo the Unfinished, In(de)finite and Unpredictable City.

Tokyo is the fourth title in Academy's highly successful World Cities series, the former three being London, Los Angeles and Berlin. Future publications include New York and Paris.

Hardback 1 85490 485 X
£75.00 $95.00 DM196.00
Illustrated throughout, mainly in colour
305 x 252 mm, 368 pages
Publication date: September 1997

LIBRARY BUILDERS

- Focuses on the current trends in library design and presents a look at the possible cyber-library of the future

- Includes nearly fifty projects from around the world by many of the world's leading architects

- Packed with hundreds of illustrations photographs, drawings and plans

This beautifully illustrated book surveys the art of contemporary library design from around the globe. As with other genres, many of today's designers, however subconsciously, draw reference from historical precedent – the circular forms of the Panopticon, the famous reading rooms of the Bodleian Library in Oxford and the British Museum, for example – but an equal number dismiss what has gone before and concentrate on the development of something 'new'.

The demand for, and the supply and dissemination of information is changing rapidly. Some predict that the book and the printed word have had their day, and that CD-ROMs, the Information Superhighway and other electronic media will take their place. *Library Builders* assesses how some designers are adapting to this change and examines the future of the library in the 21st century.

Nearly 50 libraries are presented and analysed, including Architekturbüro Bolles-Wilson and Partner's Münster City Library; Juan Navarro Baldeweg's Puerta de Toledo Library, Madrid; Sir Norman Foster's Law Faculty Library, Cambridge; Henning Larsen's Gentofte Library, Copenhagen ; Richard Meier and Partners' City Hall and Library, The Hague; Antoine Predock's Mesa Public Library, New Mexico; Dominique Perrault's National Library of France in Paris and the new British Library by Colin St John Wilson.

This is the third title in the successful 'Builders' series. The other published titles are *Museum Builders*, *Theatre Builders* and a fourth title, *Church Builders of the Twentieth Century* is due for publication in October.

Hardback ISBN: 1 85490 484 1
£45.00 $75.00 DM147.00
Illustrated throughout, mainly in colour
305 x 252 mm, 224 pages
Publication date: April 1997

Bologna 15th - 19th October 1997

INTERNATIONAL BUILDING EXHIBITION

SAIE is one of the great international building fairs that few can afford to miss. Which is why last year no fewer than 162,500 visitors converged on Bologna from all over the world. This year SAIE is preparing to meet the requirements of its 1,800 exhibitors with 200,000 sq.m. of display space, where a comprehensive line-up of building materials and services will be arranged in sectors. Yet SAIE also stages over 50 conferences and meetings during the show, offering professionals an exceptional opportunity to examine and discuss technical, environmental and land policy issues which will continue to be closely connected to the growth of the market over the coming years.

EXHIBITION SECTORS:
PLANNING, ORGANISATION, SERVICES.
BUILDING SYSTEMS.
BUILDING ELEMENTS AND SUBSYSTEMS.
MATERIALS AND PRODUCTS.
MACHINERY AND EQUIPMENT FOR THE INDUSTRIAL PRODUCTION OF BUILDING ELEMENTS.
MACHINERY, INSTALLATIONS AND TECHNOLOGIES FOR THE BUILDING YARD.
SPECIAL MACHINERY AND EQUIPMENT FOR CIVIL ENGINEERING WORKS.
AUTOMATION AND CONTROL SYSTEMS.
CLIMATEC: EXHIBITION OF AIR CONDITIONING AND LARGESCALE CLIMATE CONTROL SYSTEMS.

SAIE 97

Fiere Internazionali di Bologna Ente Autonomo/SAIE - Viale della Fiera, 20 - 40128 Bologna - Italy
Tel. 051/282111 fax 051/282332 - Internet : http://www.BolognaFiere.it/SAIE - E-mail : dir.com@bolognafiere.it

FRONTIERS: ARTISTS & ARCHITECTS

BRUCE MCLEAN, MIXED MEDIA CONCEPTUAL SKETCH FOR THE BARNSLEY ART SQUARE PROJECT WITH JOHN LYALL ARCHITECTS

Architectural Design

FRONTIERS: ARTISTS & ARCHITECTS

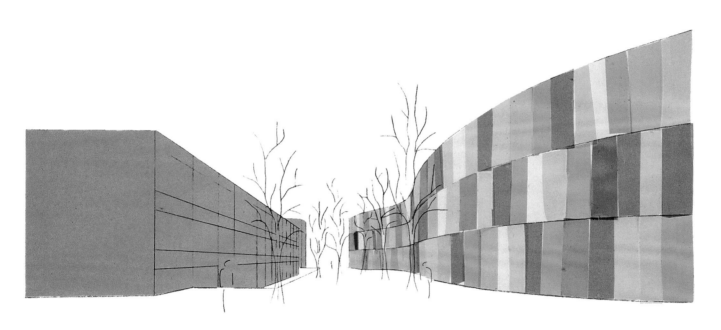

SAUERBRUCH HUTTON ARCHITECTS, PERSPECTIVE OF THE PHOTONIC CENTRE, BERLIN

ACADEMY EDITIONS • LONDON

Acknowledgements

We are grateful to Esa Laaksonen of *ARK*, the *Finnish Architectural Review*, and Michael Bond, Art Production Manager for James Turrell, for permission to reproduce the interview and images on pp76-79. Thanks to Hollands Licht, Lighting Designers for the Science Museum Wellcome Wing project, for permission to reproduce the images listed below.

Photographic Credits: all material is courtesy of the authors and architects unless otherwise stated. Attempts have been made to locate the sources of all photographs to obtain full reproduction rights, but in the very few cases where this process has failed to find the copyright holder, our apologies are offered. Virtual Artworks/Steve Bedford *pp3, 44 above right*; Peter Durant/Alex Beleschenko *p8*; Mario Bettella *pp16-23*; Barbara Gladstone Gallery *p24*; Roderick Coyne *p36*; D. Sundberg *p39 centre and below*; Dieter Leistner/Architekton *pp46, 48 above, 49 above*; Werner J Hannapel *pp49 below, 51*; Stefan Müller *p50*; Hollands Licht *p44 above and below left*; Charles Collett © MJP *p44 background*; Richard Davies *p58*; Andrew Hutler *p62*; Barbara Gladstone Gallery *p76 below*; John Cliett/Whitney Museum of American Art *p79 above left and right*; Nancy Calderwood/Musée National d'Arte Moderne; Lepkowski Studios *p84*; John Riddy *pp86-87*; Richard Wilson/Matt's Gallery *pp92-93*

Front Cover: James Carpenter Design Associates, Dichroic Light Field, laminated, textured and semi-reflective glass in anodised aluminium frames
Inside Covers: MacCormac Jamieson Prichard, Science Museum Wellcome Wing, model in laminated blue glass with blue resin interlayer and expanded metal sun shade photographed in artificial sun test
Page 2: William Pye, *Antony Cone*, Antony House, Cornwall

EDITOR: Maggie Toy
EDITORIAL: Ellie Duffy, Ramona Khambatta, Jane Richards
DESIGNER: Alex Young

First published in Great Britain in 1997 by *Architectural Design* an imprint of
ACADEMY GROUP LTD, 42 LEINSTER GARDENS, LONDON W2 3AN
A division of John Wiley & Sons

ISBN: 0-471-97695-4

Architectural Design Profile 128 is published as part of
Architectural Design Vol 67 7-8 /1997
Architectural Design Magazine is published six times a year and is available by subscription

Distributed to the trade in the United States of America by
NATIONAL BOOK NETWORK INC, 4720 BOSTON WAY, LANHAM, MARYLAND, 20706

Printed and bound in Italy

Contents

MAGGIE TOY
EDITORIAL

'Only those who have been taught how to grasp the comprehensive coherence of a larger design, and incorporate original work of their own as an integral part of it, are ripe for active cooperation in building', Walter Gropius stated in The Bauhaus Course of 1935 where a dual education was encouraged to enable the students to achieve the reunion of all forms of creative work and become the architects of a new generation. Gropius considered the architect to be an artist whose intellectual education proceeded hand-in-hand with practical training; he argued that a building designed and carried out by one man cannot achieve more than a superficial unity but that success in building is where each collaborator contributes something he has devised himself. Art and architecture are therefore inextricably linked but frequently each discipline has its own view of just how its designs should be assessed. Others have argued that the restrictions of a comprehensive functional brief remove the possibilities of artistic licence from the built form and that art is the result of a more indulgent obsession which, whilst reaching the emotions of many, will not restrict and alter the working and living patterns of those experiencing it. So the debate about architecture's position as an art rages as contentiously as ever.

This issue looks at the differences and similarities between the two disciplines and attempts to make some definitions from which the differences can be assessed. The arguments run significantly deeper than the enforced installation of 'art' in the correct position within a building to the concepts of working in unison to achieve a common goal. Four organisations of art and architecture collaborated to run a series of events during 1997 in London, instigated by Richard MacCormac who presented his call for closer collaborations. Robert Maxwell demonstrated the continuing links in the development in art and the progressions in architectural design throughout this century. He drew many wonderful comparisons, such as the work of Le Corbusier and Terragni with Boullée and Ledoux, and Hans Scharoun with Wenzel Hablick. The argument of architect as artist was also reaffirmed as he described the work of Zaha Hadid who does not compromise with conventions but behaves as an artist.

The symposium proceedings reinforced both the positive and negative aspects of disciplines working together. Many interesting points were left unraised as artists who participated unfortunately felt that they were not a part of the discussions covered. Bruce McLean, alongside Will Alsop, exuded the energy and vitality which can evolve from beneficial collaborations. The series of projects we have chosen to publish shows a range of levels of collaboration from Ian Ritchie, who frequently works alongside other disciplines to Brian Clarke, an artist who regularly works with architects; from James Carpenter, a sculptor whose many projects are developed with architects to the partnership of architect Cezary Bednarski and artist Peter Fink.

It is, in fact, fashionable to shun the labels of artist and architect. This is an interesting move but it is also important to recognise when working as a collaboration just what the role of each player is without being bound by it. The amount that can be learnt from each other in a team, as Gropius outlined, highlights the advantages of having an array of disciplines working together. This then touches on the interdisciplinary role of architecture and the advantages of opening up to a wider idea base so that a more extensive vocabulary can be utilised. Provided that each collaborator has a clear realisation of the comprehensive masterplan for the design and understands the driving concepts, the team can function with efficiency, pooling knowledge and talent.

Compromise can sometimes produce an inferior end result but the careful pulling together of fertile minds is often rewarded by practical and stimulating spaces.

Sauerbruch Hutton Architects, Week-end House, *installation, Sophia Ungers Gallery, Cologne, September 1996*

RICHARD MacCORMAC

ART AND ARCHITECTURE

Introduction at the Royal Academy of Arts, London

The idea for a series of colloquia about relationships between art and architecture, artists and architects arose from the evidence of collaborative work in the UK, Europe and the USA and a sense that the subject is of wide, even urgent interest to artists, architects, engineers, landscape designers and clients. There seems to be a number of reasons for this: one is the shift, which artists have made, out of the studio/gallery into the public realm and into the expanding arena of 'public art' and, at a deeper level, this exploration of new contexts and media may be a manifestation of a more general tendency for artists and architects to explore new territories.

The motives that architects and engineers have for collaborative relationships are varied but an underlying issue may be that late 20th-century British architects, with notable exceptions, have refused to develop an autonomous aesthetic discourse, that is to say an explanation for architectural intent independent of functional and technical reasons. Architects may be collaborating with artists to rediscover such a discourse and to assert authority in the territory of 'public art' but, more positively, the product of such collaborations is proving to be quite different to what either of the partners would have achieved independently and this, in itself, is enormously interesting.

So, it seems to me that this evening's event and those that follow at the RSA and RIBA, may be part of an important watershed for architecture as it addresses the other arts to search for its own wider significance.

Some previous symposia have been distracted by administrative and promotional issues, 'Percent for Art', award schemes and commissioning procedures. The real creative subject matter, so difficult to engage, gets completely submerged on such occasions. On the other hand, discussions on the arts tend to be highly unpredictable with disparate contributions working against the collective focus. So, in putting together our three events, we have sought a structure, to use a reassuringly architectural metaphor, which has been finally achieved by a rather unruly process of metamorphosis, which no doubt anticipates the tenor of the events themselves. Our chairman will have an onerous task of making consequential arguments from what are bound to be diverse contributions.

Transgressions: Crossing the Lines of Art and Architecture

This evening's speakers, Anthony Vidler, Robert Maxwell, David Dunster and Bruce McLean, will examine the context in which architects and artists currently work and the cultural professional and educational hinterland which inhibits or perhaps provokes the transgressions of the title. The contributors are either critics, theorists, academics, practitioners or combinations of these.

Distinctions today between art and architecture are sustained by educational and critical isolation with few critics confident enough – and Anthony Vidler is a particular exception – to cross the 'frontier'. This was not so during the Modern Movement; one thinks of the Purism of de Stijl, of Mondrian's 'Salon de Madame B' and the association during the 30s between Ben Nicholson, Naum Gabo and Leslie Martin and the magazine *Circle*. And going back nearly 200 years it was a painter of this Academy, JMW Turner, whose influence on an architect member, Sir John Soane, stimulated the latter's architecture of space and coloured light which I see as a precursor of the space and light art (or is it architecture?) of Robert Irwin and James Turrell today.

It is appropriate that James Lingwood should be chairing 'Frames of Mind' at the RSA because it was through Artangel, of which he is a director, that two of the most spectacular transgressions came about: Rachel Whiteread's *House* and Robert Wilson and Hans Peter Kuhn's *HG* under the arches of Clink Street which created, out of architecture, a kind of theatre of memory.

Frames of Mind

'Frames of Mind' at the RSA on April 28th, is less about context and more about personal attitudes, motives and commitments necessary to successful collaborations and to crossing frontiers. Shared vision, open mindedness, recognition of another's unexpected creativity are frames of mind that artists and architects need to cultivate in a commissioning environment that tends to reward new relationships rather than nurture existing ones.

The contributors to 'Frames of Mind' are all practitioners relating personal experiences and case studies – Kathryn Gustafson, Will Alsop, Edward Allington, myself and another, probably someone from the medium of cinema or music.

Fused

Finally, 'Fused' at the RIBA Architecture Centre completes the trilogy, which has progressed from the widest issues to be considered here, to the RSA's case studies, with a series of real collaborations taking place between 7th April and 3rd May. Three teams of architects and artists have been invited to transform three major spaces within the RIBA building in Portland Place. These workshops develop the potential to use the building initiated by Vivien Lovell in the workshop projects entitled 'Gateways to the Millennium' in 1994, which involved over 50 people from different disciplines. The teams contributing to 'Fused' are FAT (Fashion Architecture and Taste architects) and Pendle (visual artist and musician), Niall McLaughlin (architect) and Martin Richman (visual artist), Pierre d'Avoine (architect) and Diana Burrell (composer).

The first of these events, 'Transgressions: Crossing the Lines of Art and Architecture' was organised by the Academy Forum at the Royal Academy of Arts, London, on Wednesday 12 March 1997.

OPPOSITE: Jubilee Line Extension (Southwark station), model

ROBERT MAXWELL
TRANSGRESSIONS
Crossing the Lines at The Royal Academy

A rchitecture as Expression:
Can it Approach the Condition of Art?

Le Corbusier, Villa Savoye, Poissy, 1929-31
Giuseppe Terragni, Casa del Fascio, Como, 1932-36

The Modern Movement in architecture was a continuation of rationalist aspirations that first took shape in the 18th century, and the hard-edged white prisms of Le Corbusier and Terragni have roots in the pure geometrical forms of Boullée and Ledoux. The difference is that, largely through the impact of abstraction, architectural forms have been liberated from the duty to represent propriety through convention, and hence from the domination of the classical orders. But they are still temperamentally in favour of strong light and high definition – what we might call the light side of art – and consistent with the idea that art produces a radiance.

Giambattista Piranesi, Tomb of the Metelli (Antichità Romane)
Giambattista Piranesi, A prison (Carceri – Pl. VII)

However, the light side is only apparent because there is a dark side. There is another tradition that also has its roots in the 18th century but which develops in a different direction, by way of probing the limits of lightness and the edge of the dark. It may seem paradoxical that the 18th century, the Age of Enlightenment, should produce Piranesi, who was fascinated by the disappearance of the past, by ruins and by prisons but he is as much part of the Enlightenment as was the Marquis de Sade. In both we see a search for the limits of the darkness. In the succeeding Romantic Movement, this search gains in confidence and in power of expression and gives a new value to darkness, as, for example, in qualities attributed by Baudelaire to cats:

> *Amis de la science, et de la volupté*
> *ils cherchent le silence et l'horreur des ténèbres*

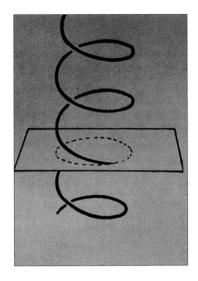

Charles Howard Hinton, Spiral Intersecting a Plane, *1904*
Marcel Duchamp, Handler of Gravity, *1934*

There is a sense in which this side of human nature has been reinforced by the development of science, with its trust in rational procedures, because it seems to attach to all those things that remain mysterious *in spite of* the discoveries of science, that is, to the unknown. The unknown is the dark edge of the known. But the rational only covers a very small domain and most of life remains outside of it. Duchamp's response to Hinton's *Spiral Intersecting a Plane was called Handler of Gravity.* In the early years of this century, scientific ideas based on N-dimensional geometry produced among artists a fever about the Fourth Dimension, analogous to our fever about Virtual Reality.[1] The unknown has always exerted a deep fascination for us, and is, in a sense, the source of all art, since art is as much concerned with disturbing order that is too complete, as with making a fresh, an as yet unknown, order. Good art of course does both.

Around the year 1907, with the development of Cubism, Abstraction began to produce forms that were no longer imitated from nature but reflected the artist's feelings in front of nature. It was Cézanne who prepared the way for this transformation. He still interrogated his motif, the evidence of his eyes, but he took certain freedoms to produce an equivalent, not a copy. He freed himself to determine the outcome by reference to his composition on the canvas, not to the raw facts. The Cubists went further in this direction. After Cubism and De Stijl, the artist's gesture was completely liberated. Art became gestural and with this new flexibility, shapes on the canvas could become the direct expression of the artist's feelings.

By the 1950s, when art began to centre on New York instead of Paris, the liberation of the gesture reached another stage. Now we see the actual marks of the paint, the gesture itself makes the final form, a form which rises through the actual movement of the artist's arm. We have reached the era of Abstract Expressionism. In fine art, the artist was entirely liberated to express feeling. In architecture, however, by what now seems a questionable development, a similar freedom from convention led to a new tyranny – the tyranny of function. The new, the unexpected, which the artist could seek inside his own subjectivity, had entered architecture from outside, from the science side; it had to be justified from a world of facts.

Hans Scharoun, Drawing for a Glass House, 1920
Wenzal Hablick, Cubic Exhibition Building, 1921

Moreover, what the artist may do gesturally on a sheet of paper has to go through a social and technical process if it is to emerge as a built work. The emphasis on expression, as opposed to a rational emphasis on the building process, has the effect of privileging the gesture over the construction; the building task may bring a certain loss of expression. It is interesting to compare Wenzal Hablick's Cubic Exhibition Building of 1921 with Hans Scharoun's Drawing for a Glass House, of the previous year. In both cases we have a glass tower, diminishing as they ascend and crowned by diagonals. Scharoun's free gesture in pen and ink has to be transposed into a set of forms suitable for building in stages. It regains its freedom by dislocation of the expected geometry.

It is a question of great interest how the impact of abstraction, which had such a strong effect in 20th-century painting, was not matched within architecture. Between the free gesture and the constructed reality lay a space: the space of functionality. Buildings had to be responsive to the uses and activities they were to shelter and had to be constructed more or less economically according to the technological resources of the times, so they tended to come out as rectangular boxes. To get round these constraints and still present the result as artistic, required an idealisation of the programme and the act of construction, and this is what gave rise to what I have called the Myths of Space and Function in the theory of modernist architecture. Both these aspects were distorted far from reality.

However, there was a brief moment in the early 20s, when architects of the Russian Revolution could claim to be both avant-garde artists and constructors of the new reality. Abstraction, which liberated the artist, began to liberate the architect.

Note
1   Hinton, Charles Howard, *The Fourth Dimension*, 1904

Bruno Taut, Alpine Architecture, *1919*
Zaha Hadid, Project: Club for Peak, Hong Kong, 1982

Today, we see a remarkable change, in which an attempt finally seems to have been made to free architectural forms from rectangular constraints, with a return to the early 20s in spirit. Zaha Hadid's drawing of 1982 for her project for a club on the Peak at Hong Kong, seems to hark back to Bruno Taut's fantasy *Alpine Architecture* of 1919. In both cases, in order to make the link between natural and artificial forms, the mountains and the buildings are merged together in the drawing. Nature is idealised in the same direction as the architecture.

In her drawings for *Planetary Architecture*, 1987, Hadid seems to be referring to Malevich's drawings for Suprematist Architecture. The drawings express an architecture that is so free it escapes gravity. It is clearly in the realm of art – abstract, weightless. The forms are light but well-defined, taken from the vocabulary of the Modern Movement. Her boldness lies precisely in the fact that she does not compromise with conventions but behaves as an artist, following her gesture. The fire station at Weil am Rhein showed that the gesture could be built, although not without somewhat changing its effect.

Konstantin Melnikov, Project – Palace of the Soviets, 1932
Daniel Libeskind, Jewish Museum, Berlin: site model, 1993-95

Le Corbusier relates how he refused a commission to design a church in the 20s because he did not see how the sort of abstract forms he was exploring could be used in a symbolic role. By 1951, when he designed Ronchamp, he had revised this view. However, the Russians embraced symbolism. In his design of 1932 for a Palace of the Soviets, Melnikov designed from the abstract to the symbolic. The building expands upwards, it consists of a pyramid accompanied by an inverted pyramid. The meaning was to cancel out the conventional pyramid with the ruler at the top and the mass of people suppressed at the base; now, the people were to be at the top; a liberation. Built form does not readily lend itself to this kind of symbolisation as in this case, the building resembles rocket launcher.

More successful is Daniel Libeskind's Jewish Museum in Berlin, a piece of modern symbolism that works through the juxtaposition of spaces. The main gallery is laid out in a zig-zag, based on part of the Jewish six-pointed star, crossing and re-crossing a mausoleum space below, into which one cannot enter but can only sense it as a forbidden world. This is potentially a very powerful way of expressing empathy.

 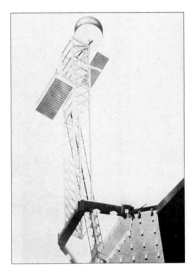  

El Lissitzky, Workshop (UNOVIS) – Speaker's Platform, 1920
Rem Koolhaas, Observation Tower – Rotterdam Project, 1982
Hadid began her career with OMA – the Office of Metropolitan Architecture – with Rem Koolhaas and Elia Zenghelis. Koolhaas is another architect who has used architectural drawing to liberate himself from convention. Here, we can compare his Observation Tower in a Rotterdam project with El Lissitzky's Speaker's Platform of 1920. So Koolhaas too takes a leaf from the Russian Constructivists, although with a preference for the purer forms of the early Leonidov. In his case, he has not abandoned the desire to build.

Rem Koolhaas, House near Paris, 1990
Rem Koolhaas, another view
In his subsequent work Koolhaas has kept quite close to the prismatic forms made canonic by their association with the Modern Movement. However, at the same time he has subjected these prismatic forms to a peculiar kind of subversion, so that instead of looking rational, they look arbitrary, the result of unconscious irony or subconscious machination. In this way, by frustrating our, by now, normal expectations of functionalist architecture, Koolhaas restores us to a world of feeling.

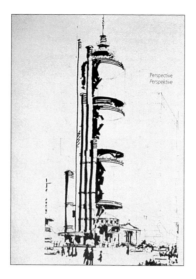

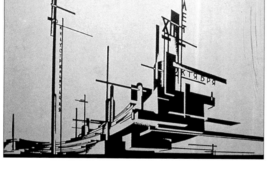

Richard Rogers, Project for Seattle, Washington, 1984
Chernikov, A Call for Industrialisation, 1929

However, perhaps on closer examination Rogers yearns for the mantle of the avant-garde artist as well. Compare his Project for Seattle of 1984 with Chernikov's *A Call for Industrialisation* of 1919, and the connection becomes clearer. Where Koolhaas returns to the heroic period in a spirit of irony, Rogers returns with his enthusiasm intact.

Coop Himmelblau, Residential Complex, Vienna, 1983
Norman Foster, Interior, Hongkong and Shanghai Bank

In Norman Foster's Hongkong and Shanghai Bank everything is apparently rational and technical, except that a good deal of accident is allowed to enter, perhaps so as to stand in for the idea of freedom, or stimulus. The space in which the escalators rise into the atrium provides us with a rich variety of juxtapositions, producing an effect which is not so far removed from the accidental look that Coop Himmelblau, the Viennese architects, deliberately cultivate as a form of expression. So the High-Tech school is slipping into the current re-valuation of expressionism.

In the modern architecture of the 20s, the attempt to bring science and technology to bear went along with rational procedures and standardisation. Today, computer technology allows all the parts of a building to be individually different. Frank Gehry pioneered computerised control of fabrication with his design for the Guggenheim Museum in Bilbao. Similarly, Nicholas Grimshaw was able to create varied parts of his Chunnel Terminal at Waterloo so that the overall form could conform to the sweep of the curves determined accidentally by the site plan. At the same time, by adopting a three-pinned arch structure, he could make the structure disappear halfway across, so that the space seems to be a result of a structural miracle instead of structural rationality. Hence, the rectangular boxes once thought to be part of rational control have given way to more sophisticated methods, and architecture is now free to follow the expressive gesture in a way it never has done before.

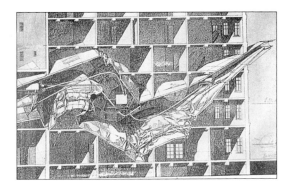

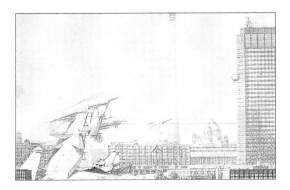

Lebbeus Woods, Berlin Free-Zone: Free-Space Section, 1990
Northern Ireland: a bomb explodes

Lebbeus Woods, an American architect of German extraction, wants to express impatience with the excessive rationality of the German State, and its tendency to impose a too rigid order, as many would see in the planning controls exercised by the city authorities in Berlin. His Berlin Free Zone – Free-Space Section makes a sharp contrast between order and disorder, and here the expression of disorder is equated with violence. What looks like disorder becomes freedom, what looks like order becomes servitude. His Zone of Freedom rips through the frame of a conventional building like a bomb exploding. On the right we have an actual bomb blast in Northern Ireland.

Lebbeus Woods, Underground Berlin, Alexander-Platz, Projection Tower, 1988
Lebbeus Woods, Lima, Peru, an improvised shanty

The image of dissolution which opposes itself to the excessive order of our presumably oppressive governments is matched by the unwanted dissolution of our cities. There is a world of difference between the forms employed by the artist to *express* dissolution and the experience of the dissolute life of a city slum, as here in Lima, Peru. To be subjected to this life where crime has become normal must be an ordeal; for the artist, to represent the forms of a dissolving order is a search for freedom. As always with fugitive meanings, we have to recognise that the state of freedom is subjective, and that the adoption of conventions so as to be able to communicate at all, while it involves a loss of subjective freedom, represents a gain in commonality and so in liberty. Architecture may approach the condition of art but so long as it is inhabited, it has other duties as well.

The forum participants

ACADEMY FORUM

TRANSGRESSIONS: CROSSING THE LINES OF ART AND ARCHITECTURE
Extracts

The extracts below were taken from the Academy Forum discussion at the Royal Academy, London on 12 March 1997 which followed the symposium on the relationship between art and architecture. Participants included the symposium speakers Robert Maxwell, Anthony Vidler, Richard MacCormac, Bruce McLean and David Dunster and speakers from the floor. The discussion was chaired by Paul Finch, Editor of The Architects' Journal.

Paul Finch: Recent events have demonstrated that the subject of this symposium is as topical today as it has ever been. The Department of National Heritage has just published a report on the desirability or otherwise of a national architecture centre; it concludes that such a centre is not necessary, that there are plenty of buildings where architecture is displayed and exhibited, and that it would make much more sense – in terms of lottery funding – to set up an endowment and to start funding some serious shows: to invest in curating rather than yet another building. On a more positive note, the same report discloses that the Trustees of the Tate Gallery are committed to extending their activities to architecture as a result of their own, very large new building down on Bankside. The Royal Academy itself is also engaged in the delicate matter of trying to persuade the Government that it should be given – or at least leased on a peppercorn rent – the rooms in Burlington Gardens in order that they be transformed into architecture rooms, thus restoring the relationship between art and architecture that was integral to the Royal Academy when it was founded. On the educational front we read that St Martin's School of Art is going to be teaching and lecturing on architecture, though it will not have a formal architecture school as such. Also at the moment, a series of art works is invading 36 Bedford Square, around the AA, and we hear that something similar will shortly be happening at the RIBA as part of Richard MacCormac's initiative; there is an apparent wave – if not tidal wave – of enthusiasm and initiative for combining these allegedly separate disciplines. In the case of schemes like the Baltic Flour Mills, a £19 million lottery project to convert a flour mill in Gateshead into a palace of art – which, incidentally, involves spending £6 million on air conditioning in a building which apparently flourished perfectly well without it when it had flour in it – one sees that most traditional of art and architecture relationships: a bit of art stuck on the outside (in this instance a rather ingenious neon arrangement which involves a set of parallel neon tubes with one deflected 10 degrees so that when they shimmer and flicker, it will appear as if the entire Baltic Flour Mills are floating off either towards or away from Gateshead). So it seems a very timely occasion to review the relationship between these two elements, and I'd like to start by asking Richard MacCormac to respond to what he's heard from the speakers this evening.

Richard MacCormac: I rather dread the task of interpreting such a concentrated series of presentations and arguments. However, it is probably most straightforward to deal with them in the order in which they were delivered, and I will try to perceive some continuities between them, which I think there were even though the speakers didn't exchange texts beforehand.

Starting with Robert Maxwell, I liked his idea of polarity, one that is not just architectural but that concerns enlightenment; enlightenment and the aspect of darkness. He mentioned Piranesi; Piranesi was the architect of memory – something which came up in Anthony Vidler's subsequent submission – because his idea of memory was centred around the excavations in Pompeii and the mythical reality that was stronger than the present. Robert proceeded to set up a series of antipathies or polarities which we experience as architects: on the one side consumerism, rationality, tyrannies of fact and science, and the difficulties of a constructed rather than an imaginative reality; on the other side the fine artist, able to find independent significances, and in the past able to articulate the Sublime, to investigate the unknown, and to achieve an abstract freedom. Robert then suggested that it is possible to conflate these polarities and that there are a number of people working in the Modernist tradition who have managed to do so, from Melnikov and the Russian Constructivists to today's architects such as Zaha Hadid and Daniel Libeskind, who are artists but still have some difficulties with the constraints of constructed reality, and Rem Koolhaas. Then he introduced an important idea: the notion of architecture as potentially metaphorical and empathetic. Having talked about Koolhaas, Richard Rogers and Gehry, and Gehry's application of his ideas through computing, he concluded that the new expressionism in architecture allows it to embrace something that it avoids on the whole: strangeness. Underlying his paper was the notion of architecture approaching the condition of art.

Anthony Vidler inverted that because he wanted to talk about art approaching the condition of architecture, and one of his subjects was Mike Kelley. He also introduced the theme of architecture's capacity for allowing us to find our cultural memory, something I found very pertinent as I've been involved with designing a building for the Ruskin Archive and Ruskin's ideas on the subject.

For me that was an extension of architecture, a move away from the very obstructive idea of spatial syntax that has been engendered by the Modern Movement, one that doesn't have attributes to it, that's meant to be an abstract experience. I found very poignant the notion that space is a medium for memory in Mike Kelley's work, and for a kind of blocked memory in Rachael Whiteread's work, as it is in Daniel Libeskind's Jewish Museum in Berlin.

Anthony Vidler also pointed out the extent to which artists have started producing works on a scale that architects had previously considered their preserve; these moves by artists into the realm of large-scale installations and spaces is quite a fierce

Mark Cousins

Richard MacCormac

critique of the assumptions that architects have had about the nature of space. Vidler developed this notion of psychologies of memory and uncertainty, talking about the lost presence in Rachael Whiteread's Vienna Memorial – which relates to Kelley's lost pasts in his work. These ventures into areas that architects thought they inhabited, I found very, very interesting. There were phrases in Vidler's talk like 'the architectural unconscious' and 'the enclosure of blocked memory' which will stick with me – particularly because of the Ruskinian connection – and he ended with an architect's venture into realms similar to those of Kelley and Whiteread: Peter Eisenman's Holocaust Memorial in Berlin, where he spoke of spatial anxiety.

In his contribution, David Dunster set up an antipathy between architecture education and art education which arises from his own experience as an educator. I always find David very profound and difficult to understand, but he established some quite real political issues, which have something to do with a certain place called the RIBA, and which arise from a conflict between the fear that is induced by the intellectual notion of architecture and a very, very hard-pressed profession: a kind of fear of art. I think these papers have been about not what you do but the environment in which you do it. The public art movement has quite frightened some architects because they wonder whether their role has been taken over – and of course they deserve it if they've retreated into utilitarianism, to go back to Robert Maxwell's introduction. There is a fear of intellectual activity and of the power of art. David talked about rejoining this but also built up a picture of some sort of cultural conspiracy (I didn't quite understand this), which inhibits the rejoining and encourages the students to understand their position in relation to the media which defines the world we live in. For that reason he was suspicious of the symposium's title, because 'Transgressions' accepts in a way that it shouldn't the polarisation between architects and artists.

To move on to Bruce McLean, one of the important points that he raised was that in Macintosh's Glasgow School of Art an environment existed where architecture and the fine arts cohabited; indeed, this was true of most similar institutions until the late 1950s. In its 1958 Oxford Conference, it was the RIBA which decided to remove the architecture schools from the art schools, to put them into the universities and to make architecture into a pathetic imitation of science. Of course the scientists didn't like that with the result that the architecture schools hang on uncomfortably in the universities – they're not very respectable really and they have difficulty coming to terms with this. I assume that we all agree that architecture is an art and that the arts should be taught

together in the same institution. Bruce showed us that he doesn't have any problems; he's clearly a completely qualified architect, doesn't need to belong to the RIBA. So that was a terrific, volcanic end to our evening. I liked his maxim: 'don't wait to be asked'.

Paul Finch: Thank you Richard. I'm going to ask a few people who didn't speak earlier to comment. Will Alsop, you've been oft-cited this evening and you paint, teach and design; what do you think?

Will Alsop: I do paint; I'm not an artist, I'm an architect, and I hang on to that title fervently. The medium that I work with is architecture and that's important. I think it's a very open medium which does allow collaborations, very natural collaborations, with people like Mel Gooding, Bruce McLean and one or two others; it's not a question of being precious. I thought it was very, very interesting that Anthony Vidler and Robert Maxwell, who gave their presentations first, tried to make sense of what was going on, and David Dunster and Bruce McLean, who followed, did not. I'm sorry David, you made perfect sense in some ways but I think that this distinction is very important because it displays a division between those who comment, think and talk about what goes on in contemporary society, and those who actually do it. I think it was very clear.

If I recall correctly, there was an axis – the western edge of the Atlantic – which came forward in your references. It was as though the other side of the Atlantic actually knows what it is and is dealing with it – only because you spoke about it so eloquently of course. I don't believe that that's so, and here there's a vibrancy which is attempting to discover what it is; the important thing for me is that these things do actually happen and shouldn't be worried about too much.

Mark Cousins: The first thing I'd like to say is that I think all disputes about disciplinary turf are absolutely infantile. However, that said, I wish that this symposium had offered a slightly narrower topic for discussion than the relationship between art and architecture, because it seems to me that, once you grant that art and architecture are both incredibly heterogeneous practices, quite incapable of being summarised, then clearly they can have many different forms of connection and many different forms of disconnection. I don't think that architecture and art can be essentialised: there's not something called architecture and something called art; it seems historically inevitable that this has happened. The collapse of the fine arts' system was accomplished in the nineteenth century, so in a sense philosophers didn't have to think about it. Kant doesn't

Robert Maxwell

Anthony Vidler

consider the distinction between the fine arts; indeed it's partly through Kant's formulations that the distinction between the fine arts gradually empties itself. There are various other traditional attempts to make an ontological distinction within and between the fine arts, such as 'architecture is for dwelling'. These 'philosophical escapades' use the notion of architecture in order to establish architectural points but what they never do is establish any artistic or architectural points. So, on the one hand, there's no fundamental distinction and, on the other hand, there is a discursive distinction between them; discursive in the sense that even if you imagine the sort of Borghesian example where someone said: 'Here is an object that has been installed, can you imagine it as an art object and then as an architectural object?'. Yes, you actually would say different things about the same object because the fact that it is physically identical would not limit the way in which it was discussed since it would be taken to refer to one set of objects if you regarded it as architecture and another set of objects if you regarded it as a piece of art. But one connection that is clear, and was evident in Anthony's and Robert's presentations, is that which arises through the investigation of a third thing: what you might call negative spaces. It's not some virtuous moving together of art and architecture because they ought to be together but rather this question of negative spaces – the underside of modernity – moves to the fore as something which intrigues both artists and architects. As art and architecture try to investigate and expose those spaces they are undertaking theoretical work which the human sciences are incapable of doing at the moment. That is to say, they may actually be making theoretical advances through the form of art production which is itself, I think, a reasonably unique situation. But of course there are any number of ways in which art and architecture are either connected or disconnected, but it seems to me you have to discuss them each in turn rather than assume them; any relationship which is assumed to be global is by the same token going to be empty.

Mel Gooding: Well, many issues have been raised as a result of this evening's colloquium; some of them concerning what one might call the architecture of time and some the architecture of space. The way in which the discourse has been conducted has led to a closure rather than an opening, simply because there have been so many complex and difficult issues raised that it makes any following conversation difficult. But one thing does occur to me and it follows to some extent from what you've just been saying: there is a distinction that can be made, in terms of David Jones' distinction between the 'utile' and the 'inutile', the

useful and the non-useful but not allowing the non-useful to be a negative term. There's no doubt that art has to do with the inutile, with the making of things which have no particular use in the sense that we attach to tables or chairs, or buildings or doors. It is concerned with investigation, with revelation. This is borne out by Georges Braque, whose work is currently being exhibited at the Royal Academy. One of his great, late maxims is 'sensation, revelation'. Art has to do with sensation, and with revelation in that sense it has to do with celebration, taking into account the notion of sacramental celebration. It has that sort of power and use within our lives. Architecture is concerned with making spaces and places that make these – what might be called, 'best things' – possible and it is at that point that they meet. We cannot possibly think that architecture is an art in the sense that painting is an art but we can see that there is a very deep connection between them; it's a connection at the level expressed by Joseph Beuys when he said that every person is an artist. We all have to live a life that is the best possible life. Architecture can make that possible; art makes certain aspects of it visible. I remember a paragraph from Jan Tschichold's great book *Asymmetrical Typography* (1933). The thing about typography for Tschichold and for all the great typographers is that it is a utile art, an art to do with use, with making possible the living of the good life, the proper life, the enjoyment of the best things. I'm going to read it: 'Many readers of this book will deny any connection between painting and typography and they will be right if they are thinking of the representative painting of the past'. He goes on to talk about the way in which even typography of the past reflects architectural forms: 'Traditional typography is much more closely related to the facade architecture of the Renaissance and its heritage of styles than to painting . . . beneath the surface there is a definite relationship between Renaissance facades and title pages in books of the same period. In the same way,' and this is the point, 'between modern typography and modern architecture, but the new typography does not derive from the new architecture, rather both derive from the new painting which has given to both a new significance of form'. I think that's a marvellous central statement within the whole Modernist enterprise about the relation between one activity and another. A creative activity to do with not the useful thing but the revelation of things, and an activity to do with the creation of spaces and places where the best things can be enjoyed.

Paul Finch: Bruce, I'd like to bring you into the discussion. There seems to be a circularity about the whole art–architecture debate because in a sense we could stop this conversation now and say,

William Pye

Vivien Lovell

'well everybody agrees that they are connected, that one is different from the other but that they have things in common; let's just leave it at that and see what happens; let's just get on and do it'. The question is why are we discussing this relationship at this particular point in time? Are we rewriting the history of this relationship because, all of a sudden, we want art to do things for buildings which until quite recently they didn't need. Maybe we do need that neon on the Baltic Flour Mills in the same way that sustainability – discussed at the last symposium – is now used as a validation for new sorts of architecture. So if you want to design a tall building in the city it's OK provided that it's sustainable, doesn't have air conditioning, and it's even better if it's got an art gallery at street level which is double height. I mean who is using who? You have said that all architects are artists; I agree that they should be, but I don't think they are. I wonder what you feel, do you see working with Will as two artists collaborating or is it an artist and an architect?

Bruce McLean: I'm an artist, he's an architect.

Robert Maxwell: He's an architect, he said he was!

William Pye: I don't agree. I think they're both artists and they're both architects, it's an intermeshing. One of the problems is that we're trying to construct these polarities. While they don't want to be, the fact is that all artists – sculptors in particular – are to some degree designers; I'm too much of a designer for my own liking.

Bruce McLean: I don't think that. Why sculptors in particular, because you're a sculptor?

William Pye: Well, because I'm a sculptor I speak from my own experience and I think I do too much designing and not enough actual evolutionary creating. I'm not making it happen as the thing happens. I remember about 20 years ago I went to an event like this where somebody asked, aren't designers and artists the same thing? Aren't we all artists? Micha Black was on the panel and he said: 'no, designers and artists are as different as chalk from cheese, they're completely different. The designer puts the thing to bed and then a manufacturer makes it.' In a sense that's what architects do. They design buildings which are then made. Every architect wants to be an artist. Architects would like to be artists – I think Will Alsop is one – and an awful lot of architects are essentially artists. It's an intermeshing of the two disciplines and the fact is that a lot of sculptors, so called sculptors, are almost 90 per cent designers. I think that Donald Judd was

largely a designer: he put the thing to bed and then it was made and experienced. I think it's just that we want to see these separate categories. Mel Gooding really struck a chord in me because I've spent this week doing something which other people might consider thoroughly functional: I've been studying a water spout, developing how water pours from it and what makes a spout. Most people would approach this from a functional direction; they would be designing a water jug. I thought I'm not going to design a water jug, I am going to design the way water pours; I'm just going to observe, completely non-functionally, the beauty, the sheer magic of water pouring out into a sort of stallion's dream.

Richard MacCormac: But you have to differentiate between design – as in fashion design – and what an artist does; certainly we are designing when we know what this thing is. We design that form in certain ways. On the other hand, there's another idea behind that which might have nothing to do with objectivity at all and we deal with that as architects. If you read Dan Sidcup in *The Guardian* on Monday, he tries to posit the question: is this art? Well it's a question that never occurs to me; whether a building's art or architecture just happens naturally *en route*.

William Pye: If you make wonderful things as a gardener you're an artist; I mean it doesn't matter.

Richard MacCormac: Yes, but that's not really the point Bill. You can't just say that architecture is design, which is what you implied, and then say that it is also art. You have to ask how we distinguish between the elements in the total complex that make human life and culture what they are. Hence we come back to something which relates to architecture, what we might call the architectonics of any given situation. Structures can be formed by human interaction or by human genius, so what we're discussing is how situations are structured and how interactions are structured.

Robert Maxwell: I think that that deals with the point David raised about the media because a lot of us could agree that human values arise within culture, but he's suggesting that they arise within the media and the media is taking over the function of culture. So it's as if culture itself if being rarefied at a low level and all the time humanity is just leaking away into the air. We're losing humanity while the media takes over our culture. That's what David is saying, isn't it?

Bruce McLean

Parvene Adams

David Dunster: Well I wouldn't use the term humanity, but I would use the term culture.

Robert Maxwell: But you used the term culture and you also used the term media.

David Dunster: Yes. My point here is simply that I agree with Mark on territorial disputes. If the discussion goes down the route of specifying the genus – whether it's art, sculpture, landscape, making cakes – then it seems to me that we have already fallen into the trap. What I'm concerned about is how to get to the point of manipulating the media. We're now in the situation in Europe, and maybe globally, where the old certainties of the nineteenth century under which art was produced, arts are produced and reproduce themselves – that those certainties are no longer with us. That is, I have serious doubts about the category of the client. I suspect that the category of the client has been taken over by the category of the curator; and I know in terms of architecture that the category of the client has been taken over by the architectural journalist. Now that's what worries me. I know quite a few schemes where the judging of designs has actually been undertaken by architectural journalists. I am worried about the power that the media has over painting, sculpture, architecture and music.

Parvene Adams: Architecture competitions are not judged solely by critics; they may be judged afterwards by what you call the media, architecture journalists or critics – they all play one role or another. But a lot of the people who are involved in architectural competitions for major commissions are architects themselves and the client certainly exists because the clients are the ones who drum up the money. Whether they are local authorities, organisations or individuals and how they are influenced is another matter; but I don't think it's true to say that there's a category of low-level journalists and critics which has this power. The real level of client involvement in architecture at the moment deals with real problems, not journalistic or media problems, but problems that are much more structural, concerning who is controlling what and where in terms of local authority, in terms of even a private developer, etc.

Paul Finch: Let's turn to you, Vivien Lovell, for a perspective on who the client is these days and how you see the relationship between the art works and the many public buildings into which you have very successfully managed to inject them.

Vivien Lovell: As far as we're concerned, the client is any body in control, with the budget for public space or public building. Of course this can vary from local authorities, development corporations, through to private sector clients in control of so called public space.

Paul Finch: Do you find that they are individuals as opposed to committees? Do you actually end up dealing with the people?

Vivien Lovell: We do end up dealing with people but I think the real problem is where there is a committee decision either behind the choice of an architect, an artist, or indeed a collaborative team to share the creative concept for a new public space. The problem with much public art now is that it is the result of a committee choice and the result of compromise. There needs to be a new role for the enlightened client and also a very clear vision that is fostered by Government, hopefully the next Government.

Bruce McLean: But who's going to do it, the architect has to; the architect has to state, to demand the client. You can't wait . . .

Vivien Lovell: I couldn't agree more, I'm not saying that one should wait at all. We need to create more opportunities for speculative proposals whether they're for public spaces, or buildings and sites of experiment where we can begin to determine what the cultural and aesthetic agenda is, rather than wait for the enlightened client. We may wait for an extremely long time.

Bruce McLean: There are no enlightened clients, we need to be enlightened by the art.

Vivien Lovell: There's a new publication currently being promoted for the Museum of Modern Art in Paris that presents unrealised projects for public spaces; indeed, there's already a similar book, *Unbuilt America*. Publications such as these are creating the climate in which one can generate and publicise these ideas, and help them to determine the aesthetic agenda for the future.

Parvene Adams: I think that Paul summarised the initial discussion by saying that we all agree. I don't think there's any agreement around this table. When you talk about Ruskin – I'm sorry, I don't know anything him – I assume that the concept of memory involved is a recovery of memory, and I think what Anthony Vidler was talking about was exactly the non-recovery of

David Dunster

Will Alsop

memory. In a sense you can play against or with it. Anthony has described the Kelley models in one particular way, as coming up against memory; Kelley didn't actually ever even try to get to the memory.

Anthony Vidler: He wouldn't touch it and I don't blame him.

Parvene Adams: Right, and with the Eisenman Holocaust Memorial there was, as it were, a work in progress but a work that was never going to succeed, to recover. You don't recover a memory: you do the work. So I think that there's a disagreement about memory around this table. In a sense I hear Anthony in a very good Freudian way, saying that there's no such thing as a memory, though I suspect that he might think there is such a thing as a recovery of memory.

Anthony Vidler: Personally I think there is, yes.

Parvene Adams: Fair enough. I just want to point out the differences.

Anthony Vidler: There's no culture without memory; all culture is memory, it's as simple as that.

Parvene Adams: Yes but you can still take the memory as a fiction and you have to go on.

Anthony Vidler: There's a certain irony that didn't come out in my talk. Because Kelley played with mutilated dolls, he had been accused of victimisation; he was a child molester or something of that kind or was himself victimised. So he figured what he wanted to do was to find out what happened, find out who was the victimiser and who was the victim; and I think what he did was to deflect the personal – his repressed family drama – into space, into inanimate forms of victimisation to assume a hypothetical scenario: OK, maybe I'm a victim – though I didn't know it – of all the formed spaces, buildings and institutional forms that I've been brought up in. Then he played out the scenario and got very serious. His initial intention was an ironic response to his critics; the actual construction took two or three years of project on project, got very serious indeed. Then I think he backed off, you're right.

Parvene Adams: Yes, but nonetheless I think you were talking in terms of space and in a sense we're talking about the body; we have to be talking about the body in architecture. There's

something else on which we differ: you were saying something about revelation, I'm not at all against the word, but then you went on to talk about the good. Now I disagree with that entirely, revelation is one thing, the good is another. Discussing Eisenman's model for the Holocaust Memorial, you introduced anxiety. Is anxiety the dominant emotion or is there something freeing about this process of working with the clues, of reconstituting the process through which the memorial was made – which is itself a work of the past in memory. This is what I understand by revelation in this context, but I don't see an extension to the public good.

Anthony Vidler: My point about Eisenman was not to do with anxiety; actually quite the reverse. On the surface the memorial is a spectacle; it presents itself as an object, and Eisenman tries to pretend that the object is revealing itself in the processes of its creation, holding its own memory inside itself, when what it really does is to make a spectacle of Eisenman's own process of creating and hermetically seals that in.

Parvene Adams: No, no, not at all. I read you completely differently Anthony; I understood you as saying that we had the clues whereby we could reconstitute or try to . . .

Anthony Vidler: He wants to give us those clues in that object.

Parvene Adams: Yes, and I was then going to ask you, isn't Mike Kelley the one who's hermetically sealed off because it's so personal and there aren't effects. When he showed the models there were no effects, whereas the Eisenman model is very powerful.

Anthony Vidler: The point was simply that I thought Eisenman was much more interested in object–object relationships than subject–object relationships or subject–space relationships and that what's interesting about the two artists I talked about (Mike Kelley and Rachael Whiteread). They are interrogating what you call a body and what I call a subject, but I think that there's some sense of investigation in the art and some sense of an inevitable kind of platitude in the architecture. You know that when the architecture tries to be art, in certain ways it can't carry it off; whether Kelley was successful in his analysis or not he was at least trying to do something quite serious. I think that Eisenman is trying to develop a process which looks as though it's like that.

Parvene Adams: Yes, but I disagree with you because I think the fact that it looks like that resonates the physical processes. So

Paul Finch

Forum in progress

Eisenman is reconstructing what you said about memory, at the level of art, architecture or whatever you want to call the model.

Anthony Vidler: His is a representational project whereas I think Kelley's has the potential at least not to be so.

Richard MacCormac: I'm glad you raised this issue. I'm not talking on theoretical levels, Freudian models, or whatever. What I'm talking about is two possibilities of experiencing what we remember and how we remember; if the good means nothing more than a feeling of well-being in the world, that'll serve for the time being. I don't mean some sort of notion of an absolute moral good or anything like that, but a sense of well-being, of us living in the world having an experience which is enjoyable.

Robert Maxwell: The sources of well-being and the enjoyable are different for every individual.

Richard MacCormac: Of course they are. This is the point I want to make. But we can certainly look at Anthony's presentation of Mike Kelley's work in which he discussed Kelley's attempt to recover a certain sort of experience and a certain sort of memory, proceeding to experience certain sorts of problems in relation to that, as a model for the whole business of whether or not it is possible to recover memory.

Then there was Bruce's presentation in which he talked about the extraordinary effect upon his life of an entirely positive kind of architectural experience: that of spending several years in Mackintosh's great school in Glasgow. This is architecture as the creation of spaces to engender the feeling of well-being, of what I called the good, I might even say the best things, as we know what the best things are . . .

Robert Maxwell: No we don't!

Richard MacCormac: Yes we do. We know that this forum is a good thing – individuals talking to each other I mean . . . Did I hear someone say architecture's not about that? Well, it is entirely about that. If it is not about that it is about nothing.

Paul Finch: I'm going to ask Robert Maxwell to have the last few words because he always expresses them more elegantly than the rest of us.

Robert Maxwell: The reason we've ended the day with a smaller discussion is that it's easier to respond to the preceding speaker and not to get stuck three or four issues back – which happened in the larger symposium where it was very difficult to sustain a dialogue. However, having said that, I find myself in a similar position now because the last three or four speakers have all said things I've disagreed with and now I can't remember who said what. So I'm in a quandary of having to sum up my own confusion.

I think that the artist knows what he's doing because he's damn well been doing it, and he says it like that – maybe he doesn't know what he's doing, but he does it and that's good enough. Will Alsop has a good understanding of that; Will Alsop is a very wiley wise guy who can work with artists but doesn't consider himself an artist, thinking of himself as an architect. He once said at another Academy Forum that his method with clients was to scare them out of their pants and then to compromise: compromise was the way. Having scared them you compromise, and at each stage of the compromise they think they're contributing; finally you get something which is OK because they have contributed to it and it's not as scary as the initial idea, though it's still pretty scary. That shows Will Alsop has a very good practical understanding of how we work.

Then there is the problem of the media, about which David has made me most anxious after tonight; the monstrous idea that in some way the media is actually exhibiting to us what our culture is. Now I'd always thought the great thing about culture is that it's only the historians who can look back with hindsight and posit, one hundred or so years later, a vague idea of what culture was then, of what influenced who; who knows whether it's true because they've all died and nobody's around who knows anymore. The historian can deal more firmly with the distant view because it doesn't change very much from year to year but on the other hand it's hazy. So the historian purveys a truth which is always after the event, always distant and always consoling in a way. But the media produces a kind of history of where we are right now, and I must say I'm beginning to feel that this is a very difficult and dangerous thing. One has to consider the way in which the media simplifies our culture, projects good or bad futures according to its view of what's exciting in a fashion: you have to have an exciting future otherwise we might as well all go home and stop wearing clothes. So David has raised a very important question tonight about the effect of the media and the way in which it seems to be taking on the role of the historian, with the advantage of being on the job, right as it's happening. Now in that situation you see the artist and the architect, they're just news. There's no difference between them, they're just news.

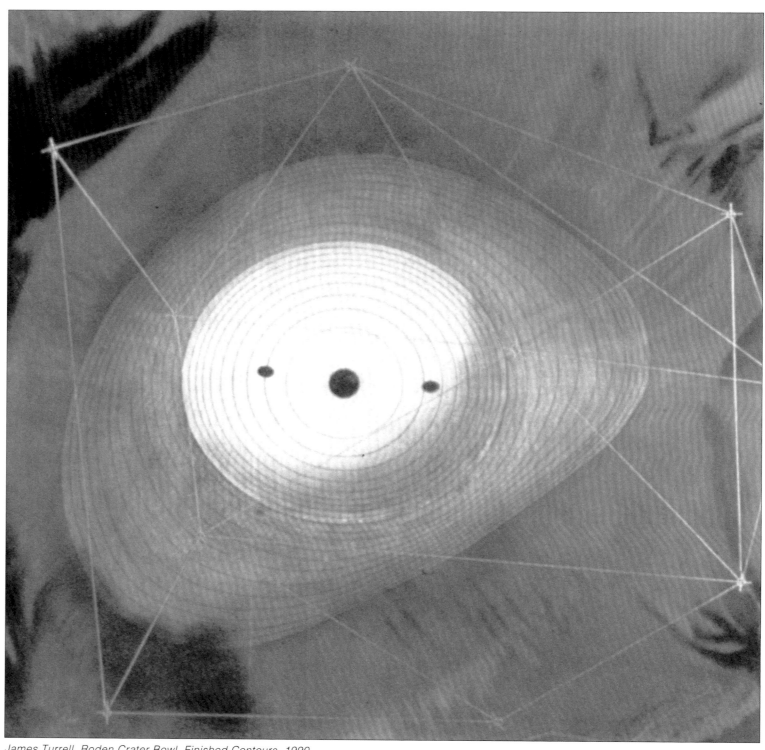

James Turrell, Roden Crater Bowl, Finished Contours, 1990

CLARE MELHUISH
ART AND ARCHITECTURE
The Dynamics of Collaboration

'Come on mates, we're artists too, we have to deal with those people outside that don't even care a damn what any of us are about', appealed Peter Cook at the International Public Art Symposium organised by the Public Art Commissions Agency in 1990. His *cri de coeur* was uttered in the face of much apparent disunity among artists and architects; the symposium organised specifically to address the problems of collaboration shortly before the Arts Council's Percent for Art scheme was instituted. It was this scheme which capitalised on the burgeoning public art movement in this country, bringing it decisively into the domain of buildings and architecture with the recommendation that one per cent of the total construction budget should be spent on art. The idea came from the United States, along with the movement itself, motivated by the desire of artists to liberate themselves from the economic and ideological constraints of the gallery system, and bring their work to a wider audience. The result was a diffusion of art practice which aimed at reintegrating art with everyday life and the city.

One of the prime instigators of what she now calls the 'ghastly public art movement' in this country during the 1980s was Isabel Vasseur, who joined the Arts Council in 1980, soon after the launch of its Works of Art in Public Places scheme (1978). The main aim was to create a better economic environment for artists, at a time when only ten per cent of art in galleries was selling to British buyers and, through a level of economic liberation, to give them a greater degree of autonomy in their work. The establishment of Percent for Art a decade later was primarily intended to extend the opportunities for artists: it was not necessarily suggesting that buildings would benefit from embellishment by works of art, or, as is now the case, that artists should be more involved in the conception of building projects from the beginning of the process, working in collaboration with architects.

However, the immediate results of Percent for Art, along with the increasing amount of public art initiated by the new public art agencies and the regional development corporations, were not very satisfactory. Many buildings and public spaces were adorned with quite inappropriate art works that were not 'site-specific' in any way except by virtue of their location. 'Some northern cities are littered with ephemeral or irrelevant pieces', says Vasseur. Furthermore, the operation of the public art agencies, she suggests, led to a polarisation of public art into a world of its own. The answer to the problem was seen to be a greater level of collaboration between artists and those, including architects and planners, responsible for the environment.

The result has been a huge proliferation of collaborative projects for buildings, public spaces and even gallery installations, which has in the last two years been fuelled by Lottery funding. The Arts Council Lottery fund, covering all forms of art including architecture, explicitly encourages collaboration by underlining the desirability of artists and craftspeople contributing to a project. Further funding for the involvement of artists in building and environmental projects has become available through schemes such as the RSA's Art for Architecture awards, or the Arts Challenge Grants for regeneration administered by the regional arts boards.

It would seem to be true to say that these initiatives have been largely motivated by the desire to improve conditions for artists and bring their work to a wider audience, rather than by a specific interest in improving the quality of the built environment, or a belief that architects and their work can fundamentally benefit by working with artists. Jess Furnie of the RSA says 'we're just' offering a different dimension'. Nevertheless the agenda is present by implication and this can and has been a source of conflict. Some architects have been offended by the suggestion that they somehow have an inadequate aesthetic sense. After seven years training they may not take kindly to Vasseur's suggestion that they could benefit from artists' ability to 'think laterally'. And for the huge number of practising architects who view architecture itself as an art, and who long for the freedom from planning regulations, building regulations, briefs drawn up by often ill-informed clients, desperately tight budgets, little public respect, and even aesthetic planning control, to produce architecture they feel worthy of the name, it is all too easy to imagine that artists are stealing that ground from them – leaving architects, in the worst case scenario, with little more than the administrative and technical side of the job. When the American artist Jack Mackie announced at the PACA symposium that 'We're in it for a level of integrity that's been stolen from the profession and science of architecture – there is a gift coming back', it was not entirely clear what he meant. Likewise, architects do not welcome the idea that, as a result of the postwar emphasis on functional determinism, survey analysis, and the plan as generator, they have lost to artists their right to exercise intuitive judgement and give reign to their creative sensibilities.

On the other hand, it is precisely this sense of deprivation on the part of many architects which has predisposed them to the idea of working with artists – 'we can slip into being more creative', says Julian Feary of Feary and Heron. At one level, of course, it is simply an opportunity – just as it has been for artists. Working on a piece of public art or a gallery installation can be a stimulating break from normal design commissions, and a chance to present architectural ideas in a different forum. Incorporating some art content into a building project can open the door not only to additional funding but also to a relaxation of planning requirements: art, it seems can break the rules in a way that architecture is simply not allowed to. Architecture is expected to underpin the establishment, while art is expected to be subversive. Above all, however, most architects believe that closer integration between architecture and art is fundamentally beneficial to the whole – and always has been in some way or another.

Art and architecture, and indeed landscape, automatically went hand-in-hand until relatively recently. The Renaissance villa was a masterpiece of integration; the great architectural theorist Alberti wrote on painting and sculpture (*Della pittura e della statua*) as importantly as on architecture (*De re aedificatoria*); while the great Baroque architects, sculptors and painters frequently interchanged roles and mediums, as Anthony Blunt demonstrates:

> Architectural members are sometimes replaced by sculpture or are so contorted and decorated that they seem more like sculpture than supporting elements. Sculptors introduce colour – almost like painters – in the form of illusionist marble inlay, by imitating the texture of velvet or silk, or by creating effects of false perspective. Painters use this last device on a vast scale and set up complete buildings on the ceilings of their churches or the saloni in their palaces. Architects execute similar effects of *leger-de-main* in three dimensions, producing, for instance, arcades which appear twice their actual length.

Baroque and Rococo, ed Anthony Blunt, Granada, 1978
The Industrial Revolution had a profound effect on the role of both architects and artists. The discovery of new manufacturing processes threatened to undermine craftsmanship and the production of art, and to open the way for the standardised production of buildings – which indeed it did. The Arts and Crafts Movement developed out of the concerns which emerged: it manifested, for the first time, a feeling that there was a need to nurture the continuing vitality and integration of the arts, crafts and architecture against the depredations of the modern world.

It is often forgotten that the entire Modern Movement, a few decades later, was founded on a vision of 'the new building of the future, which will embrace architecture and sculpture and painting in one unity . . .' (proclamation of the Weimar Bauhaus, 1919). The Bauhaus taught fine art, applied art and architecture and promoted a teaching system based on stimulating individual creativity through making collages of different materials and textures. It is paradoxical that this sort of approach has been favoured in some of the more experimental architecture schools in this country recently, while rejecting the conventional architectural drawing, or the 'plan as generator' as a modernist anachronism. The emphatic equation of modernism with functionalist dogma since the 60s has obscured the fact that modernism in architecture was powerfully influenced by Cubism in painting and its radical rethinking of two-dimensional space and form.

Modernism was built on a long historical relationship between art and architecture, but at the same time they were growing apart, asserting a somewhat resentful autonomy of each other. The professionalisation of architecture was designed to safeguard standards but it was also, in effect, a defensive mechanism designed to keep others out of the building process, which has now been consolidated by the increase of regulations and liability. Simultaneously, the rapid technological developments in the construction industry, and the standardisation of building systems, led to a heightened emphasis on the 'scientific' and technical side, as opposed to the 'art' of architecture. Meanwhile, art had long rejected its scientific basis in geometry, as it was understood in the Gothic period, and the symbolic representational role which it played throughout the pre-modern era. As a result, its traditional patrons were replaced by the commercial gallery system, and its traditional audience by dedicated 'experts' who visited galleries. What remained of public art was reduced to the level of propaganda, often in conjunction with architecture, in the hands of powerful, repressive political agencies during a turbulent period of world history. Outside this highly controlled domain, the overlap between art and architecture was gradually reduced to the physical structure of the gallery itself. Eventually that too became a source of conflict, as artists accused architects of dominating art with design.

The public art movement of the 70s was born out of the recognition that the gallery system represented a cul-de-sac, and out of the desire for free political engagement in the public realm. At the same time, modernism was failing in architecture, while socialist idealism was stifled by Thatcherite free-market capitalism, and architects found themselves in a political and economic vacuum. For two decades, the major developments in architecture were based on theoretical ideas drawn from other disciplines, notably literature, or a fetishisation of construction itself. The reaction has been a re-politicisation of architecture as an engagement with social and cultural conditions. This, combined with the instinctive desire of architects to be more creative, the collapse of the construction industry during the recession, and the result loss of normal building opportunities, has prompted a new interest in art practice as a paradigm for architecture.

According to Tony Fretton, an architect who has designed several galleries and studios for artists, art has 'an intelligence about the way objects exist politically', while 'architecture is much less willing to understand it is representing the values of society and the people it is built for'. Although he admits architecture is constrained by use, he maintains that 'art has produced much more interesting thought and form than architecture . . . said bigger things . . . in the last 30 years'. He suggests architecture has much to learn from art, but fears architects will misinterpret art practice as yet another style: 'eventually architecture will commodify and use up art', as it did with poetry and literature.

Fretton's view is very uncritical of art, a common tendency among certain architects. It overlooks the fact that much art has little or no political content (even if it does, it is not necessarily good), and it disregards much of the best architecture produced during this period; but if his pessimism is justifiable then there seems to be every reason to encourage the formation of true collaborative relationships and a more fruitful interchange of ideas between architects and artists. There has certainly been an element of faddishness in the embrace of art-derived practices in some of the schools of architecture, which one suspects has been inspired as much by the success and glamour of the young British art scene – especially by contrast with the grim outlook facing architectural students – as by a desire to express a more politicised view of architecture. But while there has been a plethora of what the cynics have described as 'third rate art', there has also been an invigoration of the architectural culture with some provocative work.

Kevin Rhowbotham was behind much of the more interesting work that came out of the Bartlett, for instance, in the late 80s and early 90s, and some of his students have gone on to operate as FAT – Fashion Architecture Taste, a young art-orientated architectural practice. Rhowbotham's concerns focused on what FAT partner Sean Griffiths describes as an intense investigation of the 'role of the drawn product in relation to architectural ideas', with a political intent. The discussion about the representation of space and the adequacy of the conventional architectural drawing to describe its occupation, generated a debate about power relations and gender politics which, Griffiths maintains, was 'the staple diet of art'. The debate stimulated an investigation of alternative means of representation, such as video and photography; computer technology – Photoshop, not CAD – had a dramatic impact, opening up a field of surfaces and iconographic elements that offered a completely different approach to architectural design from the plan-generated method.

Griffiths suggests similarities between FAT's work, using familiar elements to build up new situations and the idea of 'theming', and that of artists such as Julian Opie, Dan Graham and James Turrell, contrasting it with what he describes as the 'essentially modernist aesthetic' and legitimising values of most other architects. This tendency to relate to contemporary art as a source of inspiration representing opposing values to those of modernism is echoed by other young practices such as Caruso St John, architects of Walsall Art Gallery working in collaboration with artists Richard Wentworth and Catherine Yass. Adam Caruso states that the way contemporary art is 'installed' in a space, rather than hung formally, should be the model for contemporary architecture; he condemns modernism's aspiration to idealise and order the world, contrasting that with art's concern to 'interpret' the world, the principle of their own work. These sentiments are paradoxical in view of the parallels with modernist architects' fascination with art, manifested particularly in the influence of Cubism on the configuration of architectural mass and space. The difference seems to lie in a shift away from the fundamentally spatial concerns, aimed at physically reconfiguring the world, inspired by Cubism, towards an interest in more ephemeral forms of representation, designed to alter one's perception of the world, inspired by contemporary art.

'Most people see art as a representation', comments architect and artist Mark Pimlott, 'whereas architecture aspires to be the reality – but it often isn't; it's another form of representation'. He says it was art which opened his eyes to this. In an installation at the Todd Gallery, Pimlott aimed to reveal that 'as a place [it] conforms to certain stereotypes of what a gallery should be. It is involved not only in housing the fictional occupant of art, but is a fictional housing itself'. At the same time it is part of the city: city, gallery and art are all part of a mental construct. Pimlott's concern is to break down the understanding of architecture as a collection of facts and reveal the creation of architecture, like art, as a process of making visible the conditions in which it is made at a poetic level.

However, there is clearly a fundamental difference between art and architecture at the level of use. It is reiterated by Liza Fior of Muf, who recounts that as she and her partners – Juliet Bidgood, an architect, and Katherine Clarke, an artist – tried to work out their relationship, the question of 'use' quickly emerged as a concern shared by the architects but not by Clarke: 'Katherine said it could just be what it was'. Clarke defines her interest, as an artist, as 'the way that ideas take up existence in the world as objects or spaces'. This is the basis of the critical discussion that has come out of art practice and provides the yardstick for a definition of public art: 'if art is to exist in the public realm it has to exist critically'. But once an artist's ideas are embodied in a work of art, the process is finished: there is no further level of transmutation into a reality of space and matter defined by use and determined to a very large extent by the outside agencies of client and various authorities.

This is a complex issue which, on the whole, only a few artists seem to have addressed. For Clarke, the significant aspects of working with architects initially were the extremely precise notation of ideas through the drawing 'in a way that is completely foreign to art education', and the re-evaluation of space, in opposition to the object, as something that was not neutral but highly charged – a development that was already beginning to take place in art practice. Tania Kovats, currently working in collaboration with Levitt Bernstein on the design of the Ikon Gallery in Birmingham, funded by an RSA Art for Architecture award, was already interested in the manipulation and conventions of space, in buildings and big objects, and their effect on people, and how cities are shaped – but in a 'mainly recreational' way. She appreciated the introduction to another language and scale, while the concept of permanence implied in the proposition was both stimulating and alarming, the scope for change and substitution drastically reduced by comparison with the laboratory of the studio: 'you don't know if you've made the right decision until it's all in place'.

For artist Ron Haselden, currently working with architect Robert Barnes on a public art project funded by the London Arts Board, the appeal of architecture lies less in the opportunities it may offer to explore spatial concepts in physical terms, than in the rich field it provides for exploring human response to the built object. He actively dislikes the idea of being drawn into a collaboration with an architect from day one, preferring to be given a situation, 'like a found object', where he can 'just lay something which can change your perception of it'. Another artist again, Tess Jaray, who worked on Birmingham Centenary Square in collaboration with the city architects, describes her interest in, and engagement with architecture as being essentially visual and to do with ideas of place: 'For 30 years, architecture was one of my main sources of inspiration as a painter. The shapes, the colours, the sense of light, all came from my responses to architecture and to a feeling for place.'

Despite the apparent extent of common ground between some contemporary artists and architects, it has proved not particularly easy to forge collaborations, even in cases where there seems to be a shared outlook and goal. Part of the problem lies in the primitive preconceptions that artists and architects may have not only about what collaboration has to offer but also about each other. Architects resent being viewed by artists as technical, or 'jobbing' people (as one artist put it), lacking in creativity or intellectual ideas, and the fact that, as Ted Cullinan has put it, architecture, unlike art, is not understood as 'a central issue in the culture of the nation'. On the other hand, architects often speak with disdain of artists' lack of professionalism, naivety and inability to make decisions and keep deadlines – except for the new 'entrepreneurial' breed epitomised by Damien Hirst. Both sides seem to regard each other in equal proportion as egocentric, precious and lacking in generosity. According to one architect, there is an active dislike of architects among artists and even art administrators, and a general climate of suspicion.

Such accusations suggest there are serious obstacles to be negotiated by those interested in nurturing a collaborative relationship between the two parties. The misconceptions are reinforced by significant differences in working practice. At the PACA symposium, artist Andrew Darke stated: 'An art work has integrity because the artist is in total control, he works on every aspect in the studio.' Architects, by contrast, have to work in close collaboration with each other in teams, with their consultants, their clients and, increasingly, the general public through public consultation. They are accustomed to instructing subcontractors who will fabricate or supply the products which the architect has designed or specified. The suggestion may be that this automatically results in a loss of control and forces compromise. Many artists are not totally studio-based, and routinely employ assistants to undertake much of the hard physical labour – Ron Haselden, for example, rejects the studio approach and often designs things which are fabricated by others, preferring to 'use the outside world' – but there are many others for whom the haven of the studio and the principal of 'getting your hands dirty', maintaining the purity of the work by executing every bit personally in a relationship of close physical involvement, is religiously observed. This attitude may also be compounded by a level of possessiveness and secrecy about certain techniques regarded as highly personal which creates a resistance to the involvement of others in the making of objects.

For artists who have made the passage from the studio into the public domain, the exchange of solitude and 'total control' for the collaborative relationship and compromise, assailed on all sides by the demands of third parties, is often a shock and a challenge, but also very stimulating. It seems clear that one of the reasons Bruce McLean has undertaken so many successful collaborative ventures with architects – notably Will Alsop, John Lyall and now Irena Bauman of Bauman Lyons – is that he naturally enjoys working with other people; no doubt the fact that his father was an architect, as is his son, has created an additional level of empathy with the architect's mind. Originally a performance artist, McLean has never sought the confines of the studio, and particularly enjoys working in communities: for instance, a major part of the project for the public space in front of Tottenham Hale Station which he is working on with John Lyall is a 'Path of Knowledge' which is to be made up of work produced by children in workshops directed by the artist. However, Bauman observes that even McLean is protective of his own creativity, showing a reluctance to let assistants from her office help him in the making process at Bridlington Promenade, and refusing to deal with letters or have a fax machine – options that simply are not open to architects.

The most difficult part of any architect-artist collaboration seems to be the transition from the conceptual or design stage to implementation. This seems to be the point at which there is most likely to be conflict over definition of roles, authorship and responsibility. Landscape architect Kathryn Gustafson stressed at the PACA conference that, 'It is very important to talk about the contract between collaborators in the beginning – whether it's moral, verbal, define it well. Where's the money going? Who puts ideas down on paper?' Among artists, there is a greater freedom of notation of ideas in different media than is customary in architecture, and there may be little concept of a brief as such: according to artist Richard Wentworth, who also teaches at the Architectural Association, 'you let the work happen, you're not looking for a solution.' While the sort of architects who are attracted by the idea of working with artists are likely to be more experimental and flexible in the way they approach a brief and notate ideas, a common understanding of the role of the brief and the shared language of the architectural drawing is the basis of the architectural education system. The development stage of a collaborative project seems to provide both parties with an opportunity to explore other approaches which is generally found to be stimulating and enjoyable, rather than to engender conflict – even when, as Julian Feary says of his collaboration with Patrick Heron on a public art work in Stag Place, London, for example, 'Patrick's idea of space is completely different from ours [as architects]'. In the case of Bridlington Promenade, Irena

Bauman describes the process of developing the idea with the artist as a very 'exciting and experimental' stage; alternatively, architect Axel Burrough reports that the main medium for collaboration between Levitt Bernstein and Tania Kovats at the Ikon Gallery was discussion, avoiding the problem of notation. While this process, in whatever form, may work very well, the presentation of ideas is likely to reveal the differences in the way that architects and artists are accustomed to work. For instance, in John Lyall and Bruce McLean's scheme for the regeneration of Barnsley through public art, McLean's vividly-coloured abstract collages seem to bear almost no relation to Lyall's apparently 'fixed' architectural drawings. Underlying tensions are likely to emerge once realisation of a project gets under way. Tania Kovats – who describes herself as generally 'very pleasantly surprised by the whole experience' – observes that at the Ikon Gallery the additional pressures of construction and the need to make firm decisions led to a focus on issues of authorship which had not been evident before. This can easily undermine the basis of a collaboration, since, as she says, 'one of the attractive things about collaboration is that shared responsibility'.

For Irena Bauman at Bridlington, it made no sense that, having developed the whole concept for the scheme jointly, she and McLean were then obliged to separate certain isolated 'collaborative elements' in order to make an Arts Council Lottery funding application. Furthermore, the pleasures of the early stages of collaboration and the 'sense of freedom' she derived from working with an artist were soured by the fact that, as architect, she was contractually obliged to take responsibility for the realisation of the project and for the artist, with power to penalise him financially if need be. She hopes that in a future collaboration with the young artist, Jenny Saville, they will be able to have completely equal contracts. At Bridlington, McLean himself had to take out substantial liability insurance. Indeed Bauman fears that the sheer weight of contractual obligations generated by health and safety regulations could become a serious impediment to collaborative ventures of this sort in the future, since most artists are simply not in a position to take on the sort of responsibilities that architects are subject to. At some point, she warns, someone will take someone else to court, and 'it will change the whole nature of collaboration'. Bauman suggests that if the gallery could expand its traditional remit as the artist's agent to encompass a new role in this sphere it would be a significant step forward in safeguarding the continuing viability of collaborative ventures.

This year, art and architecture collaborations have reached their apogee, celebrated in a whole series of different events at the main London arts institutions. In the glare of publicity, however, an important reality has been obscured, and that is that art and architecture are merely generic terms, each covering a great multiplicity of manifestations inspired by an enormous variety of intellectual and artistic interests. There is a danger in elevating the desirability of collaboration between architects and artists to the level of an ideal *per se*, independent of any interest in, or proper understanding of the motivation that lies behind the production of art and architecture by individuals. Although there are people who would support the idea of collaboration for its own sake, this seems to suggest an investment which has little relation to the real basis of collaborative relationships: a coming-together of minds, with a desire to pursue common interests for the sake of the work and the role it might take up in society.

Irena Bauman, Bridlington Promenade, chaise longue designed in terrazzo to match artist's material

Tania Kovats, Ledge, 1995, paper, resin, steel frame, 250 x 200 x 150 cm

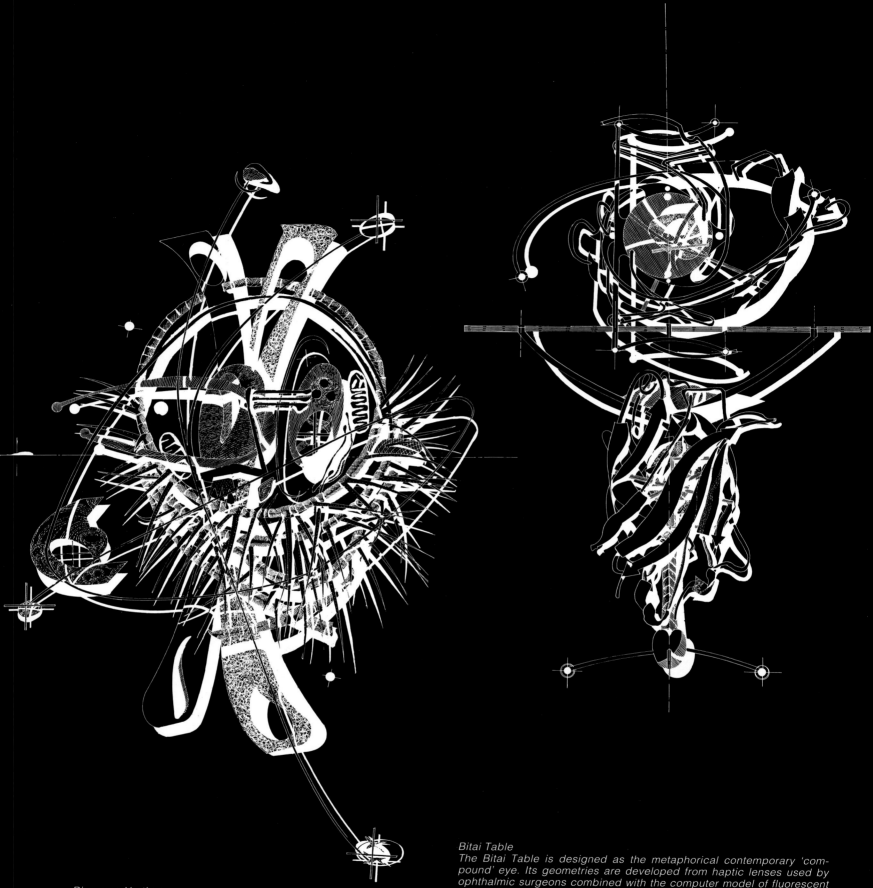

Bioscape Vertigo

This is an attempt to transcribe some aspects of the new landscape and the geometries of the new conic 'un' sections of vision. It is without scale and without navigatable order. The traveller in its nested dynamics teeters on the edge of Bioscape Vertigo. The relationship between parts is not snapped to any Platonic conspiracy. The architecture of the cell is held and supported by the 'Extended Phenotype'. DNA is the new crucifix and a religious reading is possible; the thorns are not an accident . . .

Bitai Table

The Bitai Table is designed as the metaphorical contemporary 'compound' eye. Its geometries are developed from haptic lenses used by ophthalmic surgeons combined with the computer model of fluorescent protein. As well as the word play of 'BIT' and 'AI', bitai is Japanese for 'sexual allure'. The changing eye is still a useful symbol for the effects of digital and soft technologies but this new eye like the new flesh will be hardly recognisable. This new eye is the synthesised amalgam of organic and mechanic, wet yet dry, binary yet analogue and focused everywhere simultaneously. Its cone of vision is no longer conic; the conic sections of perception are bent out of shape and of a higher order topology. It is simultaneously fluorescent and luminates all it scans with hyperreal exactitude.

NEIL SPILLER
ARCHITECTURAL GUILT

Occasionally in its advance the artist's hand turns full circle to embrace a form or note an image that had flashed through the mind – only to proceed thereupon to another point where a new landmark is to be erected. Here and there small signposts gradually give rise to areas in which particles of shells or man-made tools oppose their cluttered existence to the emptiness of the plains . . .
March 1963 Nicolas Calas from the catalogue 'Exhibition of Gouaches and drawings by Yves Tanguy', March 26 – April 13 1963, Pierre Matisse Gallery, 41 East 57 Street, New York.

'Form follows Function', 'Truth to Materials' and other such calls for architectural censorship still echo around my head attempting to curb the architectural sinner in me. The worry starts every time I set out to design, paint or make something, 'What is it and why is it useful, will it be expensive?' This rationalist modernist sensibility was burned into my soul by a provincial architectural education which sought to teach me how to feed the system with unquestioning mundanities. Even now the guilt and excitement of flagrant nonconformism sends shocks of shrill pleasure through me as I throw out deformed shapes and summon the ghosts of symbolism. I wage constant battles against the warrior monks of whiteness, those crusaders against dust, rust and the slant, whose habits are beautifully sewn but which only mask total nakedness. These disciples of the orthogonal are willing supplicants to their clients/Masters of the Universe as they burn in their bonfire of vanities.

I am an architect; this gives me great pride but also great pain. Conventional wisdom dictates that architects are the servants to their clients, providing the necessary professional expertise with which to realise their wishes. I am afraid I am not that kind of architect. This begs the question of what type of architect I am, or indeed if I am an architect at all? All my documents say I am: none tell me I am an artist or a writer. In the early 90s I wrote about my work in terms of a blurred boundary: 'An Interstitial is a drawing that is neither art nor architecture: it is a graphic means of exploring an idea and allowing randomness to influence the conception . . . the poetic drawing teaches us the notion of "betweenness": between architecture and art, between reality and fiction, between black and white. In a continually changing world, this seems an advantage.' It is this idea of change that is forever throwing up new areas of research. The arena of my work is always shifting as I hang onto the coat tails of the technological imperative, leading me into strange worlds, which at first seem much removed from the world of the professional architect. Architecture is the yardstick with which I measure and learn about the world. My trajectory has made me familiar with Fractal geometry, virtual worlds, machine ecologies, the arguments for and against Dolly the sheep and the joy of 'sketching' in steel. These lessons and thoughts provoke and enable my architec-

ture both to form and be expressed. It is in these obsessions that the elusive thing, 'the personal architectural lexicon', becomes developed and debated. I encourage my students not to follow the vagaries of fashion or the sycophancies of style but to create a language of architecture that is personal to them, an architecture that operates and is composed with reference to their individual way of seeing and being in the world. The first few steps in this new and, at first, bare world are full of fear. The call to renounce sophist dogma and the traditional architectural brief with its retarded view of the world and humanity is greeted with a sickening reaching out for hackneyed abstraction and fruitless analogy. Paradoxically, it appears that technology holds the key to the students' intellectual paralyses. This technology is not the technology of Le Corbusier or of the Baroque Master of Hi-Tech. It has little to do with the machine aesthetic and even less to do with the sparsity of mass production and economies of scale. Students can easily accept the idea of the progress of science yet become incredulous once its full pace is revealed to them. They are happy with a concept that can guarantee faster Game Boys but are shocked by the ontological changes that such a pace of innovation brings. Nonetheless, I believe architects' and architecture's central purpose is to create environments that exploit these continually new found technological opportunities in ways that satisfy the demands of human comfort or titillation; the sublime harnessed to the ridiculous one might say. Whilst my work is consistently referred to as art, I prefer to believe its guiding force is that of technology. But then again, how would I know? I am only the author.

Obviously technology is but one aspect of the complexities within art and architecture. The idea of the architect/artist as not fully in control over his work/design is not a new one. This issue of the author's ambivalence as to the exact status of his own work is crucial in creating a dynamic and symbiotic relationship between product and designer. Something weird happens when one creates without forethought. Conventional architectural wisdom does not trust the playful making of marks or the joyful juggling of shapes unless it is to satisfy some initial concept to which every subsequent move must adhere to. It does not believe that totally unpredictable product could have the same status as a predictable one. There is a critical and creative mind in the artist, and the exceptional one balances the needs of both.

The making of work that is not controlled by the conscious mind frightens architects, who are trained to be the ultimate control freaks. It seems that as technology grinds on, architectural control becomes a thing of the past. The materials of the future will not always remain in the dogmatic configurations but will readjust to liberate users from the crippling inertness of today's architectural form. My work, I hope, is about the art of architecture in an accelerating technologically mediated future. But then I am also of the opinion that the artist/architect usually invents an explanation for the work after it has been created.

MICHAEL SPENS
ART CONCEPT, ARCHITECTURAL PROCESS

The difficulties with the purely conceptual have always been those of verification, consummation and ultimate fulfilment. The necessary exchange between concept and process has to be formalised within precepts of continuity. Colin Rowe drew our attention to the essential copulation of ideas as long ago as 1975, by quoting Samuel Johnson:

> Wit, you know, is the unexpected copulation of ideas, the discovery of some occult relation between imagines in appearance remote from each other. And an effusion of wit therefore presupposes an accumulation of knowledge stored with notions which the imagination may cull out to compose new assemblages.[1]

Within this continuum of opposites, we have learnt to recognise the Sublime, even if reminded of it to excess in the past five years. In the context of a simulated attempt to correlate the initiatives of artists with the hesitant embrace of architects today, a field is available where synergies can be readily conjured together – that of the Sublime. As Burke recognised, concepts of the sublime infuse beauty with a codicil, a propensity with foreboding, where a hinterland of catastrophe is normative. That mood occurs in the best type of detective novel; Raymond Chandler crafted such a scenario in *The Long Goodbye*:

> I went out and left the door open. I walked across the big living room and out to the patio, and pulled one of the chaises into the shadow of the overhang and stretched out on it. Across the lake there was a blue haze against the hills. The ocean breeze had begun to filter through the low mountains to the west. It wiped the air clean and it wiped away just enough of the hear. Idle Valley was having a perfect summer. Somebody had planned it that way. Paradise incorporated, and also Highly Restricted. Only the nicest people . . .

Chandler has prepared a scenario of doom. Beauty and perfection are the veil. Even Capability Brown could not have composed things better – the lake, the hills, the haze, an Arcadian breeze – or Claude, or Poussin. The figures in the landscape are likewise incidental, in the middle ground:

> It was quite a long time before the speedboat came tearing down the lake again . . . it was almost four o'clock when I heard its distant roar swell into an ear-splitting howl of noise . . . I walked down to the edge of the lake. He made it this time. The driver slowed just enough on the turn, and the brown lad on the surfboard leaned far out against the centrifugal pull . . .

The sound, in fact, concealed the gunshot noise when Marlow's host was shot by his wife inside the house at that precise moment. The Sublime is never far from shock-horror, as Chandler's hero already knows.

In film in the 1990s, the Sublime has proliferated; whether as repeatedly orchestrated in Anthony Minghella's production *The English Patient*, or parodied in Bertolucci's *Stealing Beauty* and in contemporary art, through the work of Damien Hirst, for example, it has firmly consolidated a reflex-generating hold on

Salzburg Art Museum, Hans Hollein

Life and Death, installation at 1972 Venice Biennale, Hans Hollein

Le Grand Bleu, Will Alsop

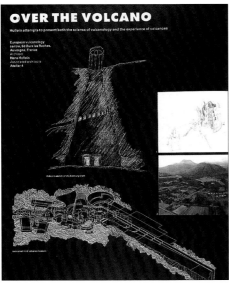

Museum of Vulcanology, Hans Hollein

current *zeitgeist*: as characteristic of the decade as the 'Picturesque' was of the cultural 'mish-mash' of the 1980s.

In architecture, a growing aspiration to acclimatise within the cognitive field of the sublime, to tolerate the symptoms of 'vertigo' that it cultivates, can be traced back to the 1970s. Such architects as Stirling, Behnisch, Piano, Hollein, Gullichsen, Pallasmaa, Coop Himmelblau and Bernard Tschumi, have been followed more recently in this direction by Bolles-Wilson, Hadid, Koolhaas, Holl and Will Alsop.

The common ground of the Sublime had, of course, been tested early on by land artists in the 1970s, including Richard Serra and Robert Smithson; both made stringent efforts to adhere, and to avoid the constant threat through critical misrepresentation, of affiliation to the 'Picturesque'. Richard Serra would claim emphatically that his sculpture *Clara-Clara* is concerned with the effect of parallax, the progress around the work of the spectator, and of formal disjunction. And Robert Smithson, similarly, would abhor the depiction of his work 'Spiral Jetty' by aerial photography as utter distortion of an experience essentially derived at ground level. The Picturesque, as such, is always lurking around, it seems, ready to appropriate artistic visions, defuse them, and render them harmlessly void of creative impulse, eliminating disjunction, disarticulation, dismay.

It is revealing to examine the work of two architects in particular, whose work is wholly different and yet in both cases ranges freely and productively across the common ground of the Sublime – a symbolic territory inhabited predominantly by visual artists, film-makers, and novelists, and mostly avoided by architects. It is by joining this common ground that both Hans Hollein (b.1934) and Will Alsop (b.1947) have developed their quite unrelated work. What they display in common is a creative attitude that refuses to acknowledge that their architecture is other than the leading edge of art.

Hollein has achieved and sustained a continual presence in this area, aided by a close correlation with installation art concepts. Other commentators have drawn attention to Hollein's concern for iconographic substitutions or inversions, and their pre-eminence in his work. There was a strong strain of ambiguity, coupled with uneasiness over the persistent appetite for monumentality amongst corporate clients. This was the time when Hollein first began to sink his architecture into the landscape. The famous Aircraft Carrier collage (1964) and Wippel House (1966) indicate this urge. The church project for Turach (1974), on a lake site surrounded by mountains emphasises identity with a horizontal 'jetty' *qua campanile*, jutting along into the lake, instead of probing the sky.

The Mönchengladbach Museum of Art (1984) has been described as a surrealistic earthwork, swelling up out of the sloping site. Today, more than ten years later, the site has greened over effectively so that a disjunctive, reactive topography is revealed with the fluid responsiveness to extraneous pressure of a bed of volcanic lava. The institution, too, appears deliberately as an institution *manqué*, but highly accessible nonetheless.

Hollein's most successful venture into a purely symbolic installation art came in 1972, at the Venice Biennale. The construction entitled *Work and Behaviour – Life and Death* was constructed at the Austrian Pavilion beside a small canal. The placement of every enclosed or open scenario was contrived with precision of thought to establish a mood of foreboding, of infinity, and of the oppositions of life and death in the human predicament. What was increasingly evident from early on was that Hollein is fundamentally a part of the continuing tradition of the contemporary sublime.

A special characteristic in Hollein's work has always come from the urge to exploit unusual site conditions, even to confound what might appear as immutable circumstances – whether of scale, or elevation, or conjunction, or typology. At Mönchengladbach, for instance, the museum appeared as several buildings. At Frankfurt, the isosceles triangle-shaped site of the Museum of Modern Art is reconciled consummately with the existing urban grain, with the entrance made at the base rather than the apex of the triangle (as convention might have prescribed) so giving the 'prow' a dramatic precedence. At Salzburg the idea of establishing an art gallery in a sunken, rock-hewn cavern has inevitable atavistic references. To expand this concept to a series of deep caves and recesses lit spasmodically by shafts of sunlight or daylight involves delving, which has profound implications for human sensibility. Hollein has offered a schema so fundamental that its seemingly atectonic condition simply re-endorses basic timeless experiential codes in a way that utterly confounds the trivialities of the Neopicturesque faction. Hollein characteristically invoked first principles here; a resolutely purifying immersion in space is prescribed, or rather a sequence of subterranean spaces to be experienced yet which cannot, a priori, be imagined.

Hollein's negation here of conventional tectonic criteria, while still deploying fundamental (albeit catacombic) means of enclosure to satisfy human requirements in the literal sense, harnesses subconscious human reflexes to being underground to advantage in optimising focus on objects, and their timeless meaning. The whole is achieved reductively, through a minimisation of the formal system of the museum as institution, hence encouraging fuller concentration on the exhibits displayed.

Hollein's more recent work, the Museum of Vulcanology currently under construction at St Ours-les-Roches, Auvergne, France is central to his importance in the progression of the contemporary sublime. Located in an area of high former volcanic activity (which has bestowed clear regional characteristics in geology and building), this museum building unites a number of Hollein's earlier formal preoccupations, and develops further the idea of the rotunda. The Museum at St Ours-les-Roches is inserted to merge with the surrounding undulations of the landscape. The complex is signalled by a great truncated cone, the *cone doré*, which is an abstraction of the extinct volcanoes outside. The remaining series of volumes are either wholly, or at least partially, submerged.

The design brief was complicated, with exhortations to remind visitors of Jules Verne, of Dante's *Purgatory*, of Plato's protective cave. 'Fire was to be present in an atmosphere both sinister and threatening, but also exuberant and joyful.' Nothing less than a 're-definition of sublimity' seemed to be demanded. Hollein has accepted this.

Visitors will penetrate an earth womb to embark on a journey of discovery to a depth of some 9 metres (30 feet). A ramp winds down round the top of a 29-metre-deep crater which belches smoke and vapour. A series of routes provides a revelation under ground, a kind of initiation into the underworld, cut through basalt. Hollein has rendered the built complex indistinguishable from the experiential totality of the site: both are one. Hollein has specified local materials such as basalt (used in the immediate vernacular building), grass and water and deploys them wherever appropriate. Many of Hollein's preoccupations of the past decade are incorporated: a ritualistic processional route; a void carved out of solid geology; conical space as core element covered by translucent or transparent rooflight or shallow dome; movement by visitors or occupants peripherally up or down a conical space (via circulation elements adjacent to the surface edge of the cone or cylinder); and external concealment of the new building by not disturbing its pre-existent surface, whether in the case of a palazzo or a fragile landscape.

Will Alsop commits himself to architecture through painting his concepts out. His best known work has always been made abroad, primarily in Germany and France, rather than at home, which is perhaps still significant in 1997. However, here I intend to address in detail only one building, where, as with Hollein, further and deliberate 'transgressions' occur between architecture and art in the contemporary sublime. This building is generally known as 'Le Grand Bleu'. It was completed in 1994, in Marseilles, France, as the regional centre of Government for Les Bouches-du-Rhône (Region No 13). The design was the result of an open competition in which Alsop beat Norman Foster into second place. The building is essentially tectonic in character, and so displays its emblematic roof apparatus boldly, eschewing any idea of weightlessness, yet embracing the play of light.

The technology transfer of lightweight panel elements with their necessary ribs, spars, skins, and incorporated hydraulic systems for the operation and control of moveable components within and without (roofs, wings and flaps) represented an aspect of sublimity which, as Burke would say, 'arouses the initial passion of "astonishment", with some degree of horror . . .', as Colin Rowe quoted Burke:[2] 'hence arises the great power of the sublime . . . it anticipates our reasonings and hurries them on by an irresistible force.' Then, noticing this:

the inferior effects are admiration, reverence and respect, and sensations of the sublime will further be induced by terror, obscurity, power, privation, vastness, infinity, succession and uniformity [which Burke designates as the artificial sublime] magnitude, light, and very importantly pain.

So we do not need the morphine, rather the valium in our contemporary dilemma.

A deliberate uneasiness becomes apparent at Marseilles after the initial Burkean tremor of 'astonishment' in the visitor's reaction on arrival at the site. The Alsop building divides very logically into the 'administratif' blocks, two in parallel, which house the staff of civil servants: and the 'déliberatif' which as its name implies, is the chamber of government, where decisions are debated and ratified. The two are linked by bridges, and escalators, housing the council chamber and its ancillary functions. The architectural denomination of the 'administratif' and the 'déliberatif' is utterly different. The space between the two parallel blocks of the 'administratif' is an enclosed atrium.

More characteristically, and of special significance here, is the looseness of parts – and of their connections. This reflects the clear 'enabling' policy pursued as idiomatic throughout the building, by Alsop and indeed the clients. Such a positive philosophy inherited by the political institutions of France was, of course, propounded by Edmund Burke in his 'other' major text, *Reflections on the Revolution in France* (1790). Burke, even then, recognised that society was an 'organic' construct rather than a mechanistic phenomenon.

Le Grand Bleu exhibits the antithesis of articulation: Alsop 'disarticulates' the *parti* of his building. It is relevant to say that the transitive verb, '*désarticuler*' (to dislocate) has no English equivalent as such. This looseness in the architecture is fine-tuned here. Such operational necessities as the wind lip at the base of the slabs, the fire flaps proposed within the stack itself, the screens and the essential walkways contribute to this idiom of adaptiveness. Just as a painter is unequivocal in choosing colour, Alsop made Le Grand Bleu a blue to match, in exact tonal and spectral colour composition, that prescribed by Yves Klein in defining what he dubbed 'International Klein Blue'. The clear suggestion of infinity was implicit in the choice.

A member of Alsop's design team described the evolution of the atrium thus:

> the imagining of the double glass walls was precise in scope and detail. All the circulation in the *administratif* blocks was contained within these. The narrow spaces would have been threaded with walkways – moving along between two apparently endless glass planes, lateral sunlight streaming through, filtered and dappled, fresh air moving freely upwards and along. He might have felt obliged to commission music in such a compelling experiential mechanism, to be played within those spaces, to complete the enchantment.[3]

At Le Grand Bleu, a concept of political, hence physical accessibility is fostered by the arrangement of elements: by clear differentiation of functional spaces and structure in a wholly tectonic apparatus; and, overall, by the idea of infinity, symbolically inferred also by colour schemata, especially on the exterior of the whole. It is, too, a curious coincidence, noted only by the politicians of Region No 13, that each '*administratif*' block stands on two parallel rows of thirteen columns each. At night this apparent symbolism glows effusively in the starlight of the *Midi* sky.

The '*déliberatif*', by contrast is separate, yet linked in, equipped with a massive sun-shielding canopy on the eastern side, removing the maximum effects of the morning sun as it burns down on the chamber of government, itself a separate identity, disarticulated from the remainder of the complex.

In the early 1990s a new realism has been evident, a search for something more appropriate to this time, more profound than the games of the 1980s. The novels of Martin Amis convey this changed mood, portraying a society in the throes of disintegration and the dispersal rather than the dissemination of wealth.

If today, looking back, it appears that the bland prescriptions of Francis Fukuyama are the logical conclusion to *Complexity and Contradiction*[4] (or indeed its corollary) compounded further perhaps in this cuisine by the elaborate metamorphoses of Lyotard, one can envisage all three suppositions as mutually supportive rather than as ultimately conclusive; supportive of, a *tendenzia*. If we rely upon CNN to validate the contemporary *zeitgeist*, we are all reminded that historical precedent supposes, to quote Fukuyama, 'the re-emergence of illiberal doctrine out of economic failure'.[5] New fundamentalisms are set to distort pluralisms now recognised as commonplace, while the homogenisation of mankind seems the inevitable result of a contemporary technology driven fast by modern economics, and enhanced by rationality; simultaneously, in debt to both Kenneth Frampton and Hal Foster, we can acknowledge the survival of a 'resistance', not only geographically-based but underpinning a culture reliant upon the issue-based assertion of political and cultural identities. As Damien Hirst said in an interview: 'you worry about your complexion but you'll be a skull in less than a hundred years.'

In the vanguard of contemporary art, the leaders such as Hollein and Alsop reach a common ground – the hazardous territories of the Sublime – today more than ever. It is here, within the context of the Sublime rather than in the cloying orchards of the Picturesque, that truly innovative creation develops, equally potently for architects, artists, writers or film makers.

This is an abbreviated version of a lecture given by the author in honour of Professor Colin Rowe at the College of Architecture and Planning, Cornell University, on 27 April 1996.

Notes
1 Dr Samuel Johnson in *The Rambler*, 25 January 1752.
2 Colin Rowe, *The Architecture of Good Intentions*, 1994, Academy Editions (London), p111, quoted from *The Works of The Right Honourable Edmund Burke*, London, 1845.
3 Michael Spens, *Le Grand Bleu – William Alsop*, 1994, Academy Editions (London), p48, J Adams.
4 Robert Venturi, *Complexity and Contradiction*, 1966, Museum of Modern Art (New York)
5 Francis Fukuyama, *The End of History and The Last Man*, 1992, The Free Press (USA).

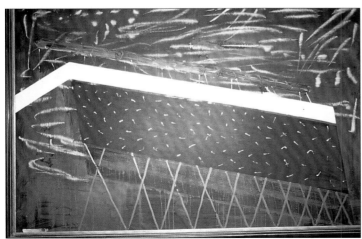

Development painting for Le Grand Bleu, Will Alsop

Le Grand Bleu, Will Alsop

Cardiff Bay Visitors' Centre

WILL ALSOP
FRAMES OF MIND

I was born in 1947. To date I am what my culture has made me, combined and mixed with a sense of my self. What culture has formed this life and this person? Post War – Baby Boom (even though my father was 64 when my twin sister and I were born) – rationing – uncertainty – a separation from Europe (from the former threat). The radio (Home Service, World Service) presented Red Skeleton and Fats Waller and the TV (bought by my parents to allow access to the Coronation) gave me *Children's Hour*. Waller to Dominoe. Haley to Elvis. (Somewhere was big Boy Cruddup). Vera Lynn lingered on but to an 11-year-old Little Richard was better. Dave Brubeck was more interesting than Chris Barber but neither were as good as Miles Davis. Culture came from America and as I became more familiar with the subject of architecture (I had wanted to be an architect from the age of six), I realised that with the exception of Le Corbusier, this too came from the States. When in 1968 I arrived at the AA in London, all eyes were on the USA: they had Mies Van de Rohe, Wright, Soleri and the Whole Earth Catalogue. Buckminster Fuller prodded the conscience and expanded the perception of architecture to an awareness of environmental responsibility; Philip Johnson never retired and we were sent Charles Jencks to tell us what was going on. Our very own P Reyner Banham even went to live there – such was the attraction of the West. This was the age of the Brain Drain and this was fed by money. My culture up to and beyond the age of 21 was in fact the culture (modified) of another country. The majority of art emerged from the county somewhere over the western horizon, the people of which started their evening when we were all in bed. My world was formed by their art, their films, their comics and their music. Life was already a collaboration. Even sex was American. The boundaries between all these activities was broken down into a soup – I was at one with this soup. Cross disciplinarianism was natural – it was the status quo. Today the problem in America is that there are no boundaries; there is no courage to accept that one discipline is different to another. There would appear to be a democratic right to allow any person to announce that they can do anything yet very few have the courage to challenge this. As a result of this the collaboration has often become more significant than the work; the means rather than the end; the process, not the result; the

sensation not the responsibility. The filling in of meaningful time, not a mission.

There is, of course, a point to cross-disciplinary work. This point is dependant on a number of issues:
• mutual respect – the architect and collaborator must know each other. The work of each collaborator must in itself present an attractive possibility to each of the parties.
• the terms of the collaboration are clearly there for the sole benefit of the collaborators. No intermediary agency must be allowed to promote collaboration. They must come from the individual disciplines themselves. In this way 'art and architecture' cannot exist without the agreement of the participants. All 'arrangers' of collaborators are leeches who take money out of the system – for nothing.
• where the will exists the opportunity exists for collaborators to discover what they do not know.

The first collaboration for the architect and the artist is with their own history. The background to ones' life feeds the work. It is only in architecture, however, that a culture has developed which denies architects the use of their experience. A code of behaviour, or manners, has evolved within architecture that has resulted in its criticism becoming self-referential. Often the code (resulting in named styles and movements) becomes very simplistic and highly accessible to the general public. This accessibility results in architecture being hoisted on its own petard. The other arts – painting, sculpture, dance, music, etc, do not suffer the rigours of public debate at the point of creation. Often artworks are rejected by the public, usually through a fear of the unknown. The architect is an artist and must be allowed to develop and test concepts and projects beyond the limits imposed by public debate. The function of a building is not a constraint. I am an architect who believes in working with the same openness as an artist. In this way I do not need to collaborate with anyone.

Curiously, because of this attitude, I collaborate with artists as a matter of course. I also collaborate with engineers, clients, acousticians, traffic engineers and so on.

The architect is free to collaborate.

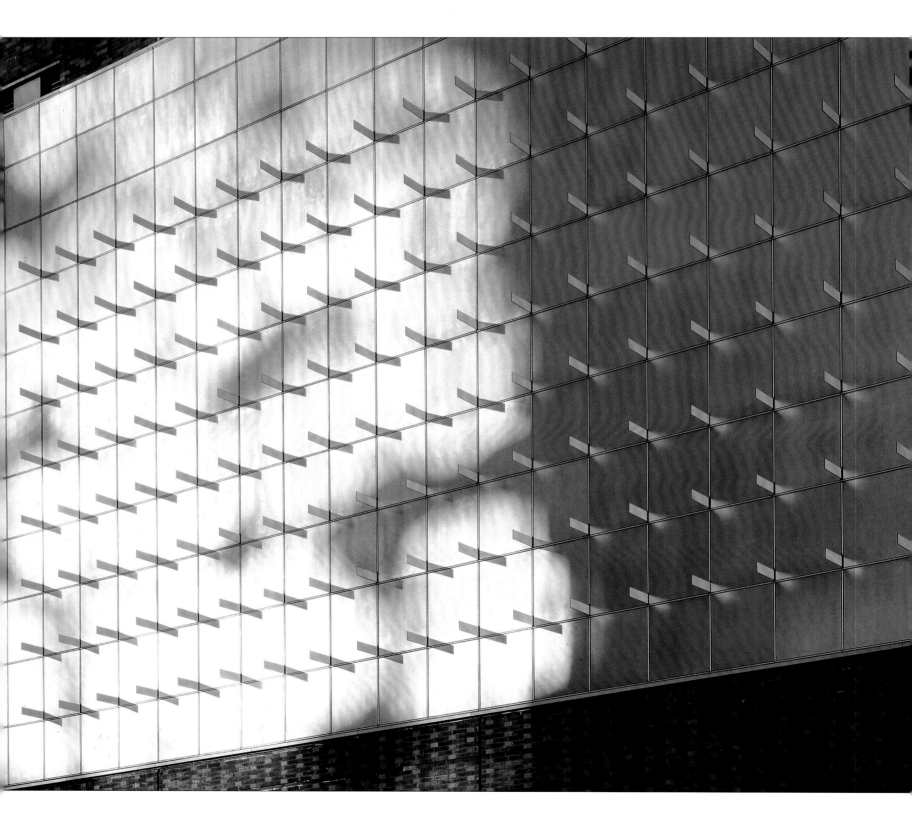

JAMES CARPENTER DESIGN ASSOCIATES

The studio of James Carpenter Design Associates, established in 1979, focuses on the exploration of light and its influence within architecture and the environment. Over the past two decades the studio has been involved in several projects that have focused attention on the public arena, of a scale that affect the population within an urban context. These have involved the interjection of an artistic sensibility within the built environment, at a scale greater than most conventional public art commissions.

The studio's method for this approach is, by and large, the design of structures which use natural light to alter a static environment. Significant projects include the design and integration of particular elements such as walls, windows, walkways and bridges into places which are made dynamic by their presence. The studio's competence in working with glass, which has involved an attempt to synthesise the aesthetic and technical aspects, has evolved over the course of 20 years, frequently crossing the traditional boundaries between architecture, engineering and the fine arts.

Most important is the studio's primary recognition that experience – whether that of people crossing a bridge, or walking along a city's pavement or passing through an airport or convention

hall – can be significantly affected by an ordered approach to the introduction of light. The design solution by the studio, especially one of an architectural or environmental scale, is often associated with the notion of a *datum*. By this it is meant that one's awareness of a place can be elevated by the insertion of an ordered structure through which the fleeting effects of light are experienced: time and movement is marked, information is revealed. Within this orchestrated experience time passes, light shifts to shadow, images appear and dissolve, colours meld and change.

At a practical level the work of the studio thus far has been afforded breadth by the opportunities presented by public arts commissions; many of them dictated by municipal or governmental budgetary requirements for public art as a portion of construction monies.

The studio, which is organised as a collaborative, is moving towards a more active design involvement in large scale public projects. Projects such as the City of Boston's Central Artery/Tunnel construction offer unique opportunities within the built environment for an intervention, such as James Carpenter Design Associates' *Light Portal*, to expand the role of art, architecture and place-making within the public arena.

FROM ABOVE: Washaba Street Bridge, St Paul, Minnesota, computer generated image; Pedestrian Bridge, Bremerhaven, Germany; Structural light reflectors, International Terminal, San Francisco Airport; OPPOSITE: Dichroic Light Field

CENTRAL ARTERY / TUNNEL LIGHT PORTAL

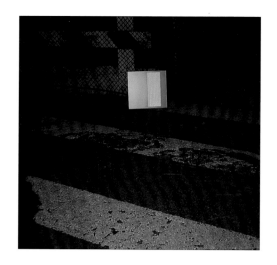

In the Central Artery/Tunnel Light Portal project in Boston, Massachusetts, a major interstate highway, which currently runs through downtown Boston by way of several undersized and outdated elevated roadways and bridges, is being rebuilt, taking the highway under the entire downtown area and creating new urban spaces and gateways into the city.

James Carpenter Design Associates was selected by the client, the Massachusetts Highway Department, to address one of the most significant gateway entrances – at the juxtaposition of the new Charles River Bridge, a monumental structure, and the highway's entrance into what will be a tunnel beneath the city. As engineered, the new 12-lane roadway, carried by the 700-foot span bridging the Charles River, slowly descends towards the ground, into which it

disappears. The space between the underside of the bridge and the banks of the river is compressed to a height of less than 15 feet, and the rectangle of land that this opening, or portal, to the tunnel occupies is over 600 feet long and almost 200 feet wide.

The studio's challenge was threefold. Firstly, to make the underbridge environment, in the client's words, 'safe, active and attractive' – the client's primary concern. Second, the studio, upon analysing the larger context involving the bridge, tunnel and river, recognised that the design would need to address and make significant the changes to the land and pedestrian ways directly surrounding the entrance of roadway and tunnel. Lastly, within the largest contextual frame, the designers saw that there were huge disparities in scale to be addressed

– from the downtown Boston skyline and cable stay bridge to passengers moving towards the city by car and pedestrians strolling through the newly reclaimed riverside and downtown parks – and that, in these disparities, an opportunity was evident. An 'aesthetic device' could be used to clarify and enhance the experience of entering and leaving the city.

It was in response to this unusual opportunity that the studio evolved a design solution that would effectively mark this intervention of highway and bridge, tunnel and boatwall, into city and pedestrian territory. The Light Portal literally forms and powerfully emphasises a datum line surrounding this new portal into the ground. Composed of 500 anodised aluminium vertical metal fins which incorporate a microprism film mounted to the surrounding concrete

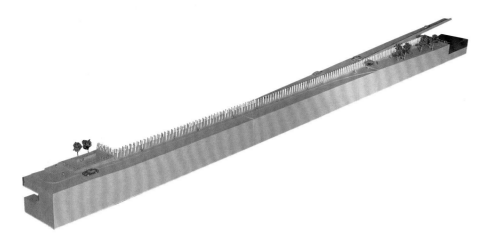

barrier walls, the portal will glow under even the low light conditions beneath the bridge and in night-time situations. The microprism film, familiar in its use for highway signage, reflects light directly back to its source and provides an economical medium for the projection of ambient light within such environmental applications.

The concept of a datum line was created by defining a perimeter that includes the long boatwalls, the passageway under the bridge and the edge directly above the 'mouth' of the tunnel. The boatwalls, which guide pedestrians down to the river, are also used as a sound barrier to protect pedestrians from the noise of the highway where the road is below grade. These walls then gradually become the barrier to the edge of the bridge as the road rises. The fins are secured to these walls; underneath the bridge, the fins are used to create not only a lit pathway along the river, but also to lead people through the space by making the very strongly ordered visual connection from one side of the bridge to the other.

Overall, the impression will perhaps be almost one of a different dimension in time – marked with subtle light from a source without clear reference, the Light Portal emphasises the idea of making a passage, uncritical of the means, from place to place. This kind of intervention is an example of the creation of a new kind of public place and experience within the context of the city.

The estimated date of completion is 2002.

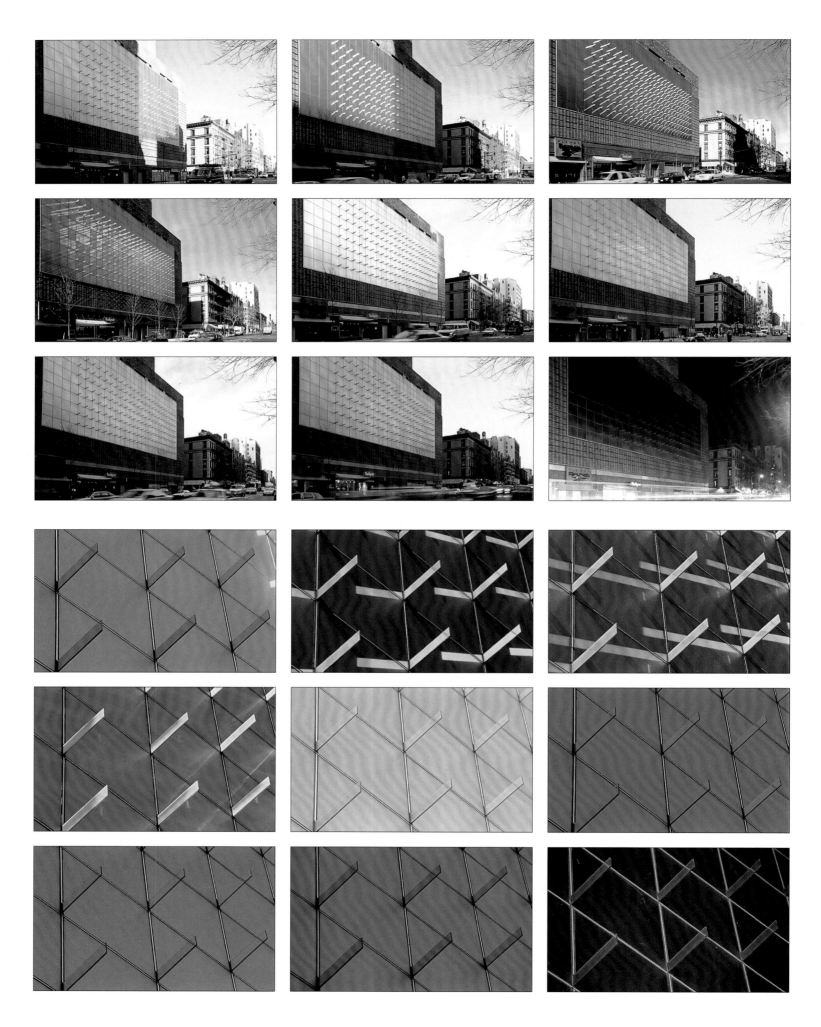

DICHROIC LIGHT FIELD

The Dichroic Light Field, a flat, gridded plane made up of glass panels and measuring 46 x 100 feet, was designed in response to a limited competition sponsored by Millennium Partnership, the developer of a new building in New York's Upper West Side, located directly opposite the Lincoln Center. This project, the winning submission, serves as an example of James Carpenter Design Associates' notions of furthering the viewer's aesthetic experience by visually engaging passers-by, and by manipulating and enhancing their experience. As 'public art' it is an unusual and somewhat unique programmatic response, at an architectonic scale and within an extremely dense urban context.

The programme called for a planar solution: the building had been designed with a large, virtually empty lower wall on the Columbus Avenue facade (inside are housed several movie theatres and an athletic club). The usable depth of the wall was very limited, thus the competition's calling for a 'mural': the expectation might have been for an applied, decorative treatment. James Carpenter Design Associates' response was to create an illusion of great depth to the wall, and to respond to the planar nature of the site by capturing the ambient light on the field's surface. Specifically, the gridded field of textured, laminated and semi-reflective glass panels is hung from the wall's surface on a simple steel substructure. The diffused surface reflects the changing light conditions of the sky, and subtly changing images. 216 glass 'fins', with dichroic glass coatings, attached perpendicular to the plane, accomplish the studio's desire of creating an illusion of greater depth and substance to the wall, seemingly disappearing into an indefinite volume behind the glass plane. The dichroic coatings on the projecting fins allow reflection and transmission of complementary halves of the light spectrum, and throughout the day they act to change the overall field of colour. When seen from the north, the field is cool – ranging from pale green to indigo; when seen from the south it is warmer, with hues from gold to magenta.

Importantly, the Dichroic Light Field enlivens the site. Changes to the proximate light – within the sky, as shadow cast from clouds, as reflections of surrounding buildings and objects – is subtly captured, and emphasised within the diffused surface of the field. In fact, the subtlety of the Dichroic Glass Field speaks directly to the often cacophonous assaults on one's sensibility within the urban context. Rather than competing for attention with neon and noise, it quietly shifts in planar images, as one moves past it and as the light of day changes with time or weather. A more refined experience is offered, eliciting curiosity, enlarging one's awareness of the introduction of natural light into the urban context.

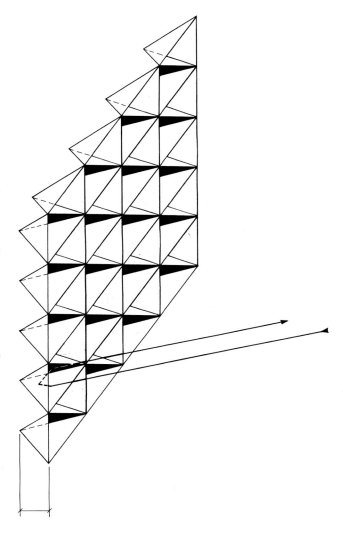

Retro-reflective sample drawing

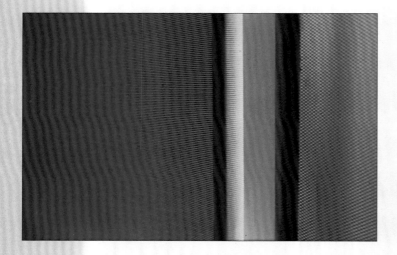

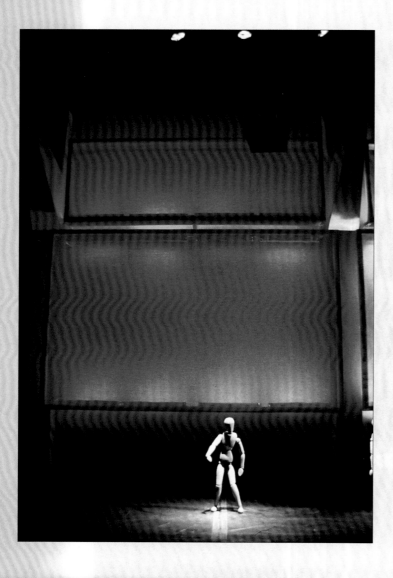

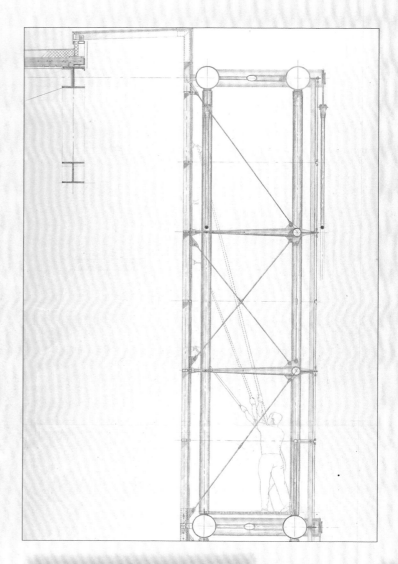

The Wellcome Wing of the Science Museum, BACKGROUND: laminated glass with blue resin interlayer and expanded metal sun shade angled towards the north in an artificial sun test; FROM ABOVE, L to R: detail of 'blue side wall' mock-up; interior view showing 'blue side walls', computer model; mock-up of 'blue side walls' at 1:5 scale; section through top part of west wall

MacCORMAC JAMIESON PRICHARD

BLUE SPACE
The Wellcome Wing of the Science Museum, London

This is a statement of work in progress towards the creation of a big blue space, perhaps the biggest blue space.

It has its antecedents, starting with Sir John Soane's *lumière mysterieuse*, his perception that coloured light disembodies, his realisation of this in parts of his museum and, most specifically, in the mausoleum of the Dulwich Picture Gallery. Soane's use of light as a coloured wash is related to his fellow Academician JMW Turner's use of glazes and washes in a dissolution of materiality which prefigures late 20th-century experiments in space and light, such as the work of Robert Irwin and James Turrell. Soane's use of colour and light amplifies a deliberate ambiguity of space definition in his architecture which places enclosing walls beyond expected boundaries.

MacCormac Jamieson Prichard have developed these ideas in various ways in recent work. In the chapel for Fitzwilliam College Cambridge, the curved, light, washed walls stand outside the space defined by the columns supporting the roof. In the intermediate concourse at Southwark Station, which will serve the Bankside Tate Gallery, the architects have worked with artist Alex Beleschenko to create a truncated, elliptical cone 17 metres high and 40 metres long at the base, consisting of 630 triangles of glass. The work is screen-printed blue and virtually opaque at the base, grading off as it ascends to near transparency, where daylight penetrates down the back of the screen. It will offer various combinations of deep blue opacity, reflectivity, translucency and transparency, amplifying the unexpectedness of strong daylight in an underground space, using the sky-colour blue as part of that inversion of expectations.

The Wellcome Wing of the Science Museum: 'Theatre of Science'

Visual and aural influences on an architect are never premeditated and only becomes apparent subsequently. In retrospect, two exhibitions at the Hayward Gallery seem to have been important for the Science Museum project – Yves Klein and James Turrell. Klein Blue is so saturated that one looks into, rather than at it, as though into space.

At the Hayward, Turrell exhibited work using light to achieve an extraordinary dissolution of boundaries, and a pursuit of evanescence which is also a characteristic of pieces by his close colleague Robert Irwin. In Britain these ventures have parallels in the work of Phao Phanit and Martin Richman.

In the Wellcome Wing project the intention in the use of colour is psychological – to create an interior which has the cool blue radiance of a night sky, to create a sense of elation and wonder (what in the 18th century would have been called 'a sense of the sublime') so as to create an appropriate frame of mind for approaching an exhibition of modern science, of biotechnology.

To achieve this the architects have appointed a Dutch firm of lighting specialists, Hollands Licht/Rogier van der Heide, to work with them and with Ove Arup & Partners on the lighting and colour in the primary fit-out of the building. The design development is being undertaken with computer models, physical models and an artificial sky and sun. The first stage has been to create a computer model of the blue west window to ascertain the performance required of its two layers consisting of an external membrane of perforated metal protecting a layer of blue glass. The objectives to be met were as follow: an internal image of blue; a transmittance of daylight which produces about 50 lux from an overcast sky within 6 metres of the window; a transmittance of a maximum of 150 lux within 6 metres of the window when the sun is shining; no sunlight penetration during opening hours; a restriction on the visible cast of blue light to within 6 metres of the window; an external image of blue at night.

The computer model established that the perforated metal had to provide complete solar protection. This allowed the blue glass to transmit enough light to appear strongly coloured from within on an overcast day and to appear blue when artificially lit from inside at night.

This has led to a series of tests using a mock-up of an artificial sky and sun combining various perforated metal screens with a range of blue glass sheets of different intensities. These physical modelling tests have established objectives which have to be reconciled. The screen necessary for total solar protection tends to conflict with the external visibility of the blue screen at night. This can be resolved with the orientation of the perforations obscuring the path of the sun but allowing visibility of the glass below the horizontal. The stronger the intensity of the glass from within and without, the stronger the blue cast into the exhibition areas. This can be resolved by limiting the transmittance to about three per cent of the full spectrum of daylight, which allows exhibition lighting levels to locally eliminate the blue cast.

Another test using physical models has been undertaken in the Hollands Licht studios in Amsterdam, where they constructed 1:5 models of bays of the interior in a simulated environment which could test the concept against a range of ambient lighting levels. Here the proposition has been to dissolve the boundary of the space by using a fabric scrim in front of a solid screen lit with cold cathode tubes using blue filters and reflectors to create an almost even spread of light. The scrim attracts focal length so that the blue lit plane behind is dislocated, appearing as an evanescent space. Blue light constitutes about 10-15 per cent of the visible part of the electromagnetic spectrum but the visual response of the eye varies depending on whether its is dark (19 per cent) or light (3.5 per cent) adapted. With effectively monochromatic blue light passing through the walls, it will be possible to project complete colour images onto the scrim which will seem to be floating on a penumbra of blue.

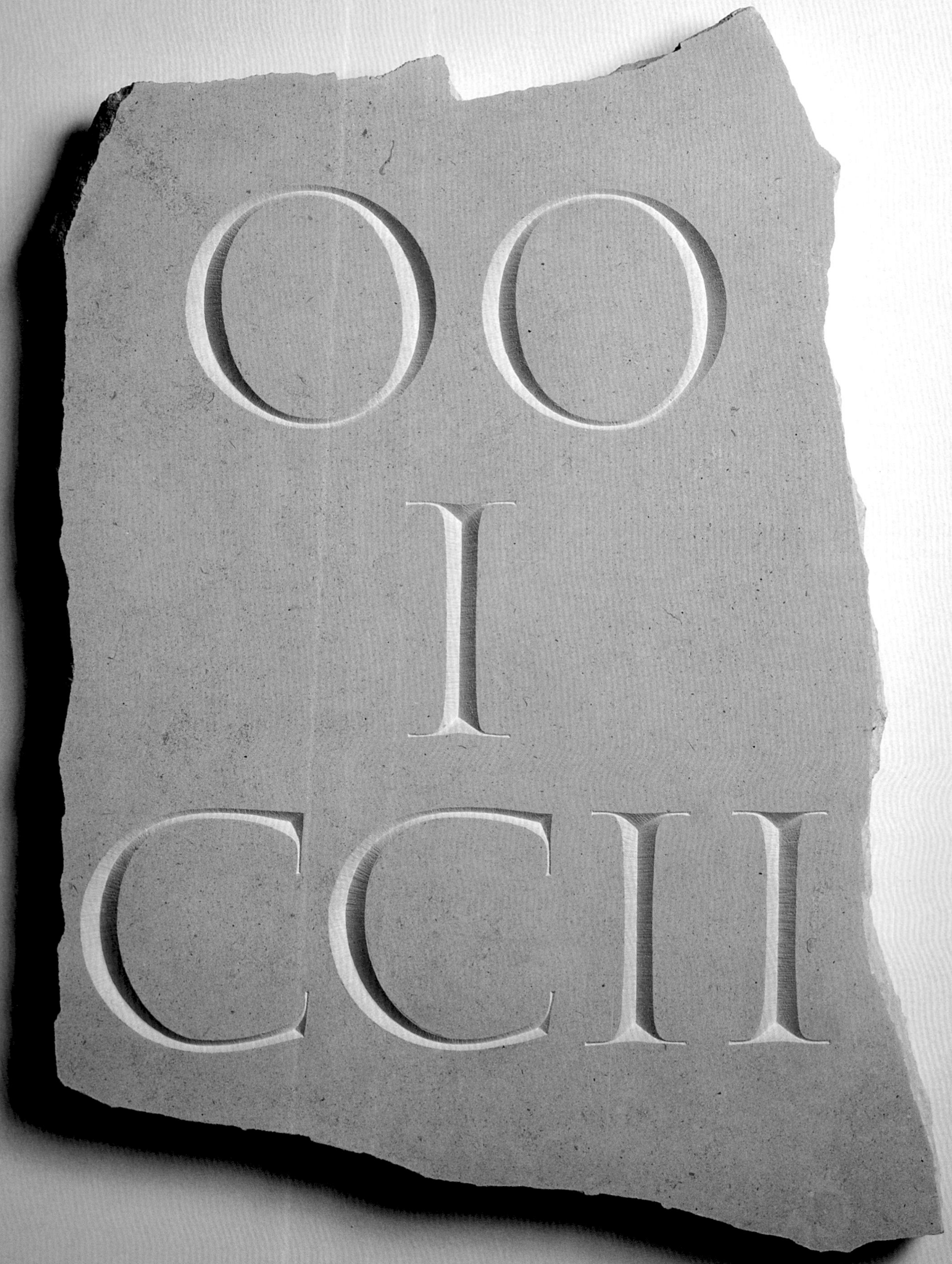
OO
I
CCII

OM UNGERS AND IAN HAMILTON FINLAY

BUILDINGS WHICH DEPICT A BETTER WORLD

A Critique by Harry Gilonis

. . . all great buildings [are] put sui generis *into the utopia, the anticipation of a space adequate to man.* Bloch

How might architecture (which Bloch saw hovering, havering, between the Extreme Box and kitsch) depict, or enact, a better world? In a text published in English in 1987, Oswald Mathias Ungers (b1926) had this to say about the 'New Abstraction':

the formal language . . . is a rational and intellectual one, not based on accidents or sudden and fanciful inspiration. Emotion is controlled by rational thinking, and this is stimulated through intuition. The dialectical process between the two polarities is almost essential in a creative process aimed towards a gradual improvement of ideas, concepts, spaces, elements and forms. It involves the process of abstraction until the object in its fundamental structure, the concept in its clearest geometry and the theme in its most impressive image appear.

(He went on to acclaim 'basic concepts of space . . . for instance . . . the four column space . . . the courtyard block . . . the perfect cube . . . ') Turning from the page to the work, we see what he means. His 1989 private library, built next to his own house in Cologne (1958-9), is a cube – known, indeed, as 'the Cube House'. The exterior skin of the building is light-absorbent dark basalt, helping to highlight the object, the concept, the structure: a pure platonic form, the simultaneous appearance of idea and building, of an idea embodied in a building.

In the light of this ethos, this practice, Ungers' collaborations with the Scots poet, artist and landscape gardener Ian Hamilton Finlay (b. 1925) can be simplistically explained: Finlay is well-known for his commitment to Neo-classicism, and that school produced, of course, powerful and revolutionary architecture obsessed with the pursuit of pure platonic forms. (Claude Ledoux is said to have built in nothing but cubes, spheres, pyramids and ellipses). But 'Revolutionary' appears above with a lower-case 'r'. Finlay is equally famous for his commitment to the French Revolution, which, far from realising any of these monumental projects actually went so far as to imprison Ledoux and guillotine his client – not for a lapse in taste, but for building (1784-87) the 46 *barrières*, tollhouses in the customs-wall around Paris. (Its breach in the night of 12-13 July 1789 was far more Revolutionary, and far more important, than the taking of the Bastille a day or so later.) Ledoux, then, was revolutionary, not Revolutionary; and for the majority of his contemporaries his tax-houses were far from being emblems of a better world. Was that implicit in his architecture? On the contrary. Bloch, an admirer of Ledoux, wrote of the *opposite* stance, Functionalism, that it 'reflects and doubles the ice-cold automatic world of the commercial society . . . its alienation . . . its human beings subject to the division of labour . . . its abstract technology'.

Ungers, a vehement opponent of the Functionalist ethos, would doubtless agree, having said that it is 'by means of formal language that function and construction are translated into art'. Of course, this is not to say that *bad* Neo-classicism cannot be inhuman, amounting as it does to the sterile incarceration of history, implicit in its conclusion (*pace* Semper) that – since style results from the harmony between a building and its historical origins – everything has already been done, and done properly. Even if the variations of form might be nearly endless (and it is perhaps impossible to conceive of them all), this still leaves the architect as the actor, if not the puppet, of history. Hardly Revolutionary *or* revolutionary. Construction in a tradition has to be more than cloning, more than the refined conclusion of sequence leaving the onlooker no part but silence. Some of what occurs in historical sequence is anticipated and continues to be relevant, and this constitutes a surplus, a continuation of the implications, open or hidden, of the cultural 'constellations' of the past. This is vitality, utopian possibility, not repetition, closure and the 'End of History'. The architect, referring to history and tradition, transforms and modifies. As Ungers has said, this is not imitation, 'for that would mean . . . that one considered history not as an existential problem, but as a series of episodes'.

We are here a long way from PoMo Heritage Architecture; as, too, is Finlay's stone sculpture *Vitruvius/Augustus – Vitruvius/Robespierre* (1986, with John Sellman). It consists of four stone blocks, to be read in sequence; these recapitulate the origin-myth of the Corinthian capital. As they grow, acanthus leaves curling form volutes; as these 'freeze' into architecture, a Revolutionary rosette appears between them. Robespierre is implicit in *pierre*; and he appears again in Finlay's work (with Nicholas Sloan) for Ungers' library. Within the four-columed space (one of Ungers' 'basic concepts'), a series of railings frame a two-storey central well, the heart of the cube. Each railing is divided by a plinth and each plinth supports a white plaster bust. Each of these represents one of (in the historian Robert Palmer's words) the 'Twelve Who Ruled'. These, the members of the Comité du Salut Public, made up the *de facto* government of Revolutionary France. Barère, Billaud-Varenne, Carnot, Collot d'Herbois, Couthon, Hérault de Sechelles, Jeanbon Saint-André, Lindet, the two Prierus, Robespierre and Saint-Just appear and re-appear in Finlay's work; not a pantheon – they were human – but exemplars. Neo-classicists often placed statues of sages and worthies in their libraries, preferring them to licentious and foolish classical divinities, Finlay concurs; the Twelve are key figures in his programme of 'Neo-classical rearmament'. Saint-Just observed that 'authority belongs not to the individual but to the law whose agent he is', so it is entirely apposite that the busts – based on an original in the British Museum – should be identical save for the

Library fragment, Karlsruhe, 1987-92

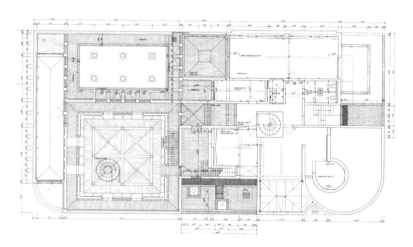

names. As similar as platonic forms, as different as individuals, they stand as a reminder that true Neo-classicism has both a history and a human face.

. . . if number, measure and weighing be taken away from any art, what remains will not be much.
                                        Plato, as quoted by Zukofsky

Ungers is adamant that the architect's chief responsibility is for *form*; 'functional principles contain no form-giving elements', which is to say, they cannot be *a priori* bases for aesthetic decisions. This flies in the face of Functionalism that finds beauty in the way technical requirements can *necessitate* form. For Ungers, as for classical architects since Vitruvius, function is subordinate – or, as Finlay put it once, 'Technology – Epic Convenience'. *Firmitas, utilitas, venustas*; structurally stable, useful (spatially appropriate) – and beautiful. Functionalism, by negating memory, risks the loss of cultural and historical values which – for Finlay equally as for Ungers – are implicit in form. Our concern, then, is not with pattern, the appearance of regularity found when any sufficiently rich structure or system is examined closely (a paradoxical lesson of chaos theory); it is, rather, with order. (The architectural pun is unintentional, but apposite; both Ungers' garden in Cologne and Finlay's in Scotland contain freestanding – that is, non-structural, non-functional – classical columns.) Such an interest in order – in *coherent* pattern – is clearly evident in the second collaboration to be considered here, the 1980-84 Baden regional library in Karlsruhe. Built from scratch as a new regional capital in 1715, much of Karlsruhe is itself ordered; much of it was laid out, in a fan shape – a Neo-classical city, radiating, if not *radieuse* – by a local architect, Friedrich Weinbrenner (1766-1826). Ungers too has spent time thinking about how to relate, to correlate, elements in a land-scape, built or natural; how to transform what he sees in order to derive the components of a vocabulary from it. As he has said, 'architecture means an analytical discussion with the environment which is developed and stamped by time'. The *Landesbibliothek* in Karlsruhe is very much a homage to the classical heritage of the city, which means in effect Weinbrenner; and much of the building is shaped by a thinking consideration of his Stephanskirche (1808-14), which faces the new library from across a road. The Stephanskirche is derived in part from Roman baths fenestration and gable – and the Pantheon – the high dome. All these elements reappear, transformed, in the library. To a naive onlooker Ungers' response might seem anachronistic, over-simplified or stark; but Neo-classical architects also pre-ferred unbroken contours, clear lines, sharp angles, wall-open-ings unsoftened by surrounds, and limited articulation of fa-cades. Weinbrenner himself on occasion used 'Tuscan', that is *unfluted*, Doric columns, in order to give a clearer, more formalised outline, adapting strict classicism to contemporary needs; he was no pedant. His first design was a rotunda rising from a cube; the church is actually cruciform with a rotunda. Ungers' building is a cube, mixing Weinbrenner's *pronaos* with the entries to two long wings to give something of the same spatial effects. The church interior has columns of the ornate Corinthian order, whereas the library's are simplified into unornamented piers, neither protruding nor recessed, smooth white plaster between openings. Ungers' interior is also referential to other libraries, including the Bibliothèque Ste-Geneviève and Smirke's round reading room in the British Museum. The interior piers bear stone sculptured reliefs (by Finlay with Brenda Berman and Annet Sterling), irregularly-shaped, regularly lettered. (There is not space here to go into the Neo-classical interest in the irregular and rough-edged, a 'natural' signifier to set against 'cultured' forms.) Each 'plaque' carries Roman numerals, with – perhaps unexpectedly – zeros. These too are not anachronisms; Hellenistic mathematicians used a symbol similar to the zero to indicate empty spaces, and the concept was carried to India, to re-enter Europe via the Islamic world. Here it hints at spans of time, extents of space, other cultures. Appositely; for the figures, translated into 'arabic' numerals, give the dialling codes for cities with major libraries – 00 30 1 Athens, 00 39 6 Rome, etc. (One might remark that these works are not as easy to decode as Ungers' building but it can be fairly said that the finer points of both emerge only with intelligent scrutiny. If neither is entirely open and giving, Finlay's remark is pertinent: 'Neo-classicism emulates the Classical while at the same time withholding itself'.) Just as fragments of classical stone inscriptions have ended up in museums, so their successors, books or scraps of parchment, are now stored in libraries; here a number-system millennia-old meets the zero, potent signifier of the computer age. In the hush of this four-storey reading room machine talks silently to machine, library to library, around the world. The ordered satisfaction of the interior is paralleled by the calm regularity of the world of numbers – 'sensual logic', in Schlegel's phrase. Yet the presence of 00 20 3 Alexandria – a library, the storehouse of a culture, burnt as fuel by the caliph Omar – might remind us of the fragility of learning, of libraries, so easily reduced, with their contents, to fragments.

> . . . *architecture's task lies in so manipulating external inorganic nature that it becomes cognate to mind as an artistic outer world.* Hegel

Ungers' work was shown at the Hamburg Künsthalle in 1984; his exhibition, *OM Ungers Architect*, combined schematic drawings on the walls with, in front of these, to scale and thus presenting an overall abstracted and sculptural effect, white plaster models. It is thus apt that he should employ the abstract, unornamented cube here too, in this, the second extension to the Künsthalle. All

Fragments of the library, Karlsruhe, 1987-92

New Künsthalle, Hamburg

three buildings occupy a raised space between two lakes, the so-called 'Museum Island'. The earlier buildings (1868/86, by von der Hude and Schirrmacher, red-brick Neo-classical; extended in 1907 by Albert Erbe, grey travertine turn-of-the-century modern) face the new building across the low truncated pyramid that makes up the courtyard. The first Kunsthalle was, in a quite revolutionary manner, lit by lantern rather than natural light on the upper floor; Ungers' building likewise has reduced upper fenestration, giving carefully-aligned views, particularly across the Innenalster and Aussenalster lakes to either side. As with the Karlsruhe project, thought about the history of the site is evident at a glance (in sharp contradistinction to projects Ungers has condemned as offering 'the anonymity of an environment based upon functional organization [where] evolved places and distinctive historical characteristics were sacrificed on the altar of the utilitarian constraints of functionalism'). Again, this is *Neo-classical* revolution; Lodoli wrote that 'ornament is not essential but accessory to proper function and form', and Perret put it more bluntly: 'ornamentation always conceals a structural defect'. The pure form has its own strengths. Pertinent here is Finlay's sculpture (one of the 1984 *Talismans and Signifiers* set, with Richard Grasby) which cites Vitruvius on the cube as a form – 'it stands firm and steady so long as it is untouched'. The new Kunsthalle again combines two of Ungers' basic spatial concepts, the cube and the courtyard, and it is in the latter, outside the building, that Finlay's contribution can be seen. Ungers has linked his design and the French revolutionary architecture of pure geometry, and it is to French Revolutionaries that we return, specifically Saint-Just. (There is a series of plaster busts of him inside the main entrance to the new Künsthalle, modelled on that made by David d'Angers, each bust bearing a quotation from his writings: these are by Finlay, with Annet Sterling again.) Guillotined after the *coup* of Thermidor, Saint-Just left behind him an incomplete manuscript, the *Republican Institutions*. In the second chapter, 'De la Société', we can read this phrase: 'La patrie n'est point le sol, elle est la communaute des affections'. Mindful of the unprecedented and committed internationalism of the French Revolution (as international in its way as the Neo-classical style it helped spread), Finlay has chosen to permute this phrase in four languages. (His 'correction' of Saint-Just's idiosyncratic *point* to *pas* only helps universalise the text.) These words, in laser-cut grey granite letters (with Berman and Sterling again), are set around the periphery of the red granite of the courtyard:

LA PATRIE N'EST PAS LE SOL SIE IST DIE GEMEINSCHAFT DER GEFVEHLE [THE NATIVE LAND IS NOT THE LAND]
ELLE EST LA COMMUNAUTE DES AFFECTIONS LA PATRIA NO ES LA TIERRA [IT IS THE COMMUNITY OF FEELINGS]
DIE HEIMAT IST NICHT DAS LAND ES LA COMUNIDAD DE LOS AFECTOS

'The native land is not the land, it is the community of feelings'.

This is absolute idealism, the idealism that reshaped a continent – 'Happiness is a new idea in Europe'. And, like all public inscriptions, it must perforce address *any* potential passer-by; not an arcane communication coded in Latin but a plain message which has, built into its form, a statement about its nature. Were the languages unmixed, or were there but one, the statement could be naive, or prescriptive; but here it has become performative, enacting however temporarily for any single reader – what it wishes to see happen. How apt this work is for an artist and an architect who both operate internationally, speaking international artistic/architectural 'languages'; as too for this site, an internationally renowned museum housing art from all over the world. Ungers has said in an interview that 'social architecture is a degree of quality (not quantity) in the design of public places . . . experienced and lived in by the community, the most important basis of identity for people in the town'. Architecture, as built environment, is unavoidable, unlike any other art; and thus must have a public ethical content – or, by denying this, implicitly negate such.

To close, Bloch again, on Hegel's definition of architecture (given above):

> architecture sees as its task to work inorganic nature into such a shape that it becomes allied to the mind as an artistically valid outside world . . . The architectural utopia is thus the beginning and end of a geographical utopia itself, of . . . the dreams of an earthly paradise. Great architecture ought to stand as a whole like a constructed Arcadia.

For Ungers, the metaphysical content of architecture lies in each individual's fulfilment and enrichment; for Finlay 'Classicism aims at Beauty, Neo-classicism aims at Virtue'. In these projects – and in others which are in process – these two attributes are inextricably melded. For, as Bloch further said – noting that architecture must 'retain man as a question' – 'hope is as old as architecture'.

Further Reading (covering the first two projects only):
Martin Kieren, *Oswald Mathias Ungers*, Artemis Verlags, Zurich, 1994
P Simig (ed), *Ian Hamilton Finlay: Works in Europe 1972-1995*, Editions Cantz, Ostfildern, Germany, 1995. Includes text by Harry Gilonis and photography by Werner J Hannappel

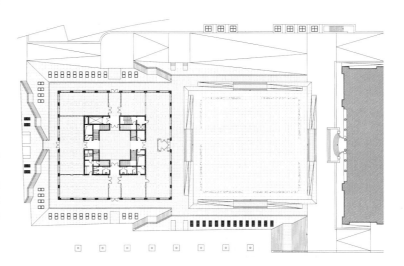

New Kunsthalle, Hamburg, FROM ABOVE: Courtyard; plan of the ground floor

IAN RITCHIE
'f' EDF V.H.V. PYLONS

'f' EDF V.H.V. PYLONS

Ian Ritchie Architects were invited in 1995 by Electricité de France to compete against seven other teams in an international competition to design a new series of very high voltage pylons – 225kV and 400kV. Other competitors included Starck, Guigiaro, Wilmotte and Perrault.

The EDF awarded joint first prize to Ian Ritchie Architects associated with RFR and Kathryn Gustafson, and Marc Mimram.

Both winning designs led to detailed design and engineering commissions from the EDF, and were prototyped during 1996. Upon successful completion of the tests, the first of the new series are being installed in France during 1997, with up to 8,000 new pylons in ten years.

The concept was developed upon a philosophical investigation into the contemporary meaning of progress. The design concept is based upon a single level configuration of the conductors, which reduces the height of pylons producing a horizontal and discreet expression. The design seeks to establish a clear spatial relationship between the lines and the topology over which it passes. To do this the architects had to develop a flexible family of pylons. Isolators can be either directed up or suspended – the latter is conventional. The pylon structural form is an 'f' carrying three phases. They are twinned to carry two circuits. The pylon column enters the ground with no detail. The principal material is rolled steel plate.

TIDAL CLOCK, CARDIFF

Ian Ritchie Architects, with the artist
Francis Gomilla, won the 1991 Cardiff Bay
International Sculpture Competition with a
Tidal Clock represented as a copper clad
figurehead.

And the bay was white with silent
light
Till rising from the same,
Full many shapes, that shadows
were,
In crimson colours came.
        Samuel Coleridge, *The Rime of the*
                    Ancient Mariner

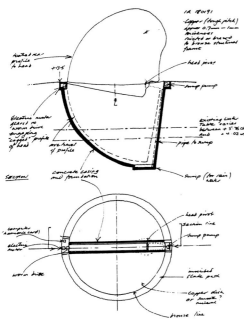

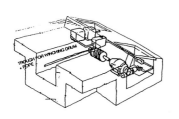

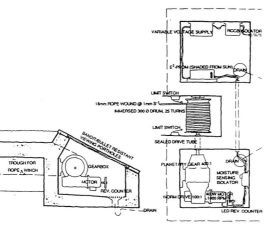

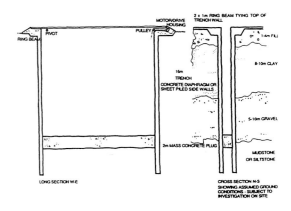

ABOVE: Derby Cascade; BELOW: Primates Gallery, Natural History Museum, London

PAWSON WILLIAMS ARCHITECTS
ART AND ARCHITECTURE
Contribution and Collaboration

In finding the solution to an architectural problem, architects have frequently used the creative collaboration with the 'usual' construction team consultants, such as structural and environmental engineers and landscape architects in order to both solve problems and to generate new design approaches. However, the opportunity for a direct design liaison with an artist during the early design stage of a building is not as commonly found and may not always be on either the architects' or clients' agenda! For, whilst in some circles architecture seems increasingly to be viewed as a technical discipline, I believe there is a fundamental problem in seeing the architect as an enabler or a technician whose labours are merely to provide functional containers which are unconnected to the world of abstract creative thought. This position would deny that architecture is an art form capable of being a creative medium in its own right, or that an architect and an artist can act collaboratively.

The following four projects by Pawson Williams describe a wide range of possibilities created by the building process in relation to the artist and their work. Each of the projects has presented design challenges which have benefited from an abstract dimension and have created opportunities and new ways for exploring ideas. The proposal for the Langdon Cliffs Visitor Centre reflects the architects' creative exploration of a series of abstract issues and their relationship to the physical world. The second project, the architects' second placed entry for an invited competition for a new theatre and music college in Argenteuil, Paris, creates the potential for a major art work as a vital component of the building's composition and organisation. The final two projects, the Primates Gallery in London and the Derby Cascade, describe two occasions where the architects worked directly with artists from the inception of a project in the development of a design concept.

Langdon Cliffs Visitor Centre, Dover Harbour, Kent
The design response for this modest building was generated by a direct response to the particularly potent location and site which sits on the edge of the cliff overlooking the English Channel. With such an exposed elemental location, the building looks to address the unique sense of place by using a spatial language and sequence to create three distinct experiences, inspired by the most powerful properties of the site – the sky, the land and the sea. The building is organised as two simple timber boxes, joined and partially wrapped by a third element, a thick masonry wall. On entering the first compartment by the masonry portal, all reference to the sea and the dramatic views are obscured. This first enclosed volume becomes a place to pause and to refocus. Having cut off the views, this windowless space emphasises the relationship of the visitor to the sky and is lit from above through a fretwork of timber screens which are oriented to exclude direct sunlight whilst allowing a halo of sky to be seen as a personal window directly above the head of every visitor.

The second stage of the sequence is contained within the volume of the masonry wall and consists of a circular ramp which slips gently into the contours of the site, creating a linear exhibition space, whilst the dynamics of the landscape and site contours are felt through the gentle descent. The earth-like material of the walls and the floor, the sloping ground and the enclosed cavelike form of this space are all intended to reinforce the feeling that one is not only part of the landscape but also almost within the earth. At the bottom of the ramp the volume opens out into the final space where the solidity of the walls drops away to reveal the panorama where the sky meets the sea in a single line between two simple blocks of colour.

Centre Régional de la Musique et de la Voix, Argenteuil, Paris
The practice was invited to prepare designs for a new music college and theatre complex as part of an overall masterplan for Argenteuil on the edge of Paris. In formulating the early design strategy, the architects were convinced that the building should offer a public focus for the area by creating the required foyer space in such a way that it would relate to the whole of the new public square and the adjacent parkland. In addition to the high degree of transparency of the foyer walls, it was proposed that the main visual focus was to be a 17 metre-high projection screen on the back wall in order to draw the eye into the building in an attempt to further dissolve the barrier between inside and outside. The screen becomes an opportunity to creatively interpret and develop the internal artistic programme of the building.

The Primates Gallery, Natural History Museum, London
Inside the main hall of Alfred Waterhouse's Natural History Building, the Primates Gallery contains the work of a number of artists and is intended to work at several levels of interpretation.

Overlooking the main hall and running the full length of the existing first floor balcony, the new gallery is a formally weighted, linear deck insertion and sets up a rigorous architectural order to define the rhythm of the new work. Bronze, glass and stone are used to place the insertion in context by using materials common to the existing building but used in an entirely contemporary manner. The new architecture acts as a framework for a series of installations and new sculpture which echoes the zoological sculptural decoration of Waterhouse's existing building, whilst setting itself apart as a clearly separate insertion. The open edge of the gallery facing the main hall has been organised in a more familiar museological manner of display cases, lecterns and text, whilst by contrast, the window wall lays down threads of man's role as a creative animal with artistic reflections on other primates in sculpture, music, film and poetry. The whole composition aims to be seen as a development of two traditions: the architectural tradition set by Waterhouse's existing building and the historic museological tradition of the museum, whilst making a third reference directly to man as the 'creative primate'. By making comparisons between mankind and other primates, the normal role of the exhibition visitor as external observer is blurred, since, in part, the onlooker is engaged in self-observation, thus gaining a sense of proximity to other primates.

Derby Cascade, Derby

Whilst the previous project was fundamentally an architectural programme with the creative input of artists included as part of the developing architectural proposition, the Derby Cascade has no functional brief to resolve and was the development of an initial idea by the artist, William Pye, through joint input. This close collaboration between artist and architect developed following a competition run by Derby City Council for a new civic feature to form part of the remodelled Market Square. It is one of a number of public art projects which have been commissioned in Derby as part of a general re-landscaping of the main public areas of the city. However, this project was unusual in that due to the scale of the 'art work', it became like a small building with architectonic qualities and considerations. The initial concept of the cascade by William Pye was to produce a curtain of water running from a bronze weir which people could walk around and see from a variety of angles. The challenge was to have a water feature which invited interaction and was of sufficient scale and monumentality to address the square. Through a process of discussion and drawing, ideas were jointly developed which looked at achieving the initial artistic goals, whilst new ideas were introduced to the work by considering certain architectural and urban issues. The development of ideas about the public interaction with the water seemed to take the place of the normal fundamental architectural concerns of ordering circulation and providing enclosure and shelter: simply put, the Derby Cascade did not become a building by involving an architect and developing architectural ideas, but remained firmly a work of art.

We have found that our collaborations with artists have encouraged a continuing re-evaluation of the design process. Architecture, like art, must be an exploration of ideas and therefore strengthening the position of architecture firmly within the arts, should be firmly on our agenda.

The following essay gives a particular view of the relationship between 'Art Product' and 'Architectural Product' through the medium of drawings. Whilst the essay can be seen as separating the artist and the architect because of why they draw, the roles are transposable, with both being common bedfellows in the pursuit of the creative ideal.

Representation and Reality: The Artist and the Architect

The works of the artist and the architect have a significant and close relationship, with both being concerned with a number of common areas – the human condition, the use of light, composition, culture, ideas and the relationship of ideas to the physical world. They will also both spend much of their time drawing. The idea that the act of drawing is a common ground which lies between the artist and the architect, connecting the purpose for which the artist will draw or paint, to the architect, is a common belief. However, it is perhaps also within this same area of potential communality that the two disciplines are divided at a crucial stage of intent. For example, the apparent relationship between the painting by Corot of Santa Maria della Salute in Venice, the three dimensional object which we know as Santa Maria della Salute and the drawings from which the building was

constructed, seem to fall neatly into categories. At first, it would appear that the two drawings are different kinds of representation of a 'real' object, and that the *building* is the only reality. However, there is another interpretation that the motivations which generate drawings, with the painting of the building and the building, have more in common than the plans from which the Salute are constructed. In order to understand how the finished building, the formal plan drawing and the painting relate – which is real and which is merely a representation of reality – it is necessary to provide a clear definition of both representation and reality.

In his book *Objective Thinking*, Karl Popper set out in the essay entitled 'On the Theory of the Objective Mind', a means of understanding and interpreting reality. Popper's theory states that there are three separate and distinguishable worlds and that reality exists within all three. The three worlds are 'the physical world or the world of physical states', 'the mental world or the world of mental states' and 'the world of intelligibles, or of ideas in the objective sense'. Within the theory, the second world, the world of mental states, acts as a mediator between the other two worlds, as the first and third world cannot interact except through the intervention of the second.

The definition of representation given by the *Pocket Oxford Dictionary* is 'a calling of attention to something, a description of something', which for our purposes will therefore relate specifically to the description of a 'third world' concept or idea in terms of a 'first world' reality, the reality of the tangible object.

Other words, whose meaning may be confused in the context of this essay and which need clarification, are architecture, building and drawing. The word 'architecture' will be used when referring exclusively to the 'third world' concept embodied in a building and the word 'building' will be used when referring to the 'third world' idea and the 'first world' constructed and tangible object. The term 'drawing' which normally means 'art of representing by line in black and white or a single colour' (*Pocket Oxford Dictionary*), will be broadened to include all of the creative two-dimensional media such as painting and printing.

It is important to make the distinction clearer between the two different types of representation which are available to describe an idea or concept. Both the building and the drawing have the potential to represent, in the 'first world', ideas which originate in the 'third world'. The distinction between the two is obvious in that they express the idea in entirely different media. A building is made up of physical material to create a three-dimensional object which is occupied and used. A drawing, on the other hand, is made up of marks on a surface and is confined to two dimensions. However, this does not make any distinction between different types of drawings – for example, the painting by Corot of the Salute would appear to be of a completely different nature and intent to those drawings from which the building was constructed. The difference between the two types of drawing has obviously to be made in another context, not associated with the physical qualities of the medium. This context is concerned with the way in which a 'third world' idea can be expressed as a tangible object which the mind can interpret and therefore understand. It is also concerned with whether the medium used is intended as a final product, capable of interpretation as it stands, or as an intermediate stage on the way to the final expression of the idea. For example, it is the building Santa Maria della Salute which ultimately represents the creative ideas and objectives of the architect. The plans and sections were never intended as the final product, only diagrams depicting the physical form and arrangement to be interpreted by the master builder, from which the final form, the creative and abstract ideas will be manifest. However, Corot's drawing of the Salute and its surroundings was not essentially trying to describe the building. His concern was with exploring other ideas within the medium of painting and hence, he was using the Salute as a tool towards that end. This then appears to give us two categories of drawing which for convenience we shall call absolute-drawing and interim-drawing.

Absolute-drawing is a drawing which is used as an end in itself and is the representation in 'first world' terms of a 'third world' concept. Interim-drawing is a drawing which is an intermediate stage on the way to the final expression and as a diagram. This category includes drawings such as plans, sections, elevations and even working drawings, all of which have one thing in common: they do not directly represent the idea but describe how the idea will be represented in the building. This makes interim-drawings a second-hand description of the idea and any interpretation of the drawing needs to take this into account. Within this method of distinction, it seems to indicate that a completed building and absolute-drawings have more in common as a method of representing ideas, than do the two distinct types of drawing. Both absolute-drawings and buildings are final products (in terms of representation) and they are chosen to express a particular idea by the artist/architect, as being the most appropriate medium for the idea.

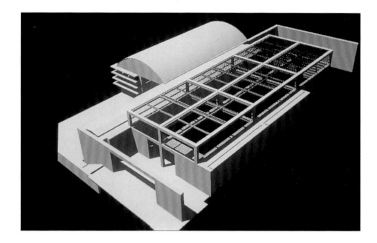

However, ideas are not mutually exclusive to the media, as it can be seen that similar abstract ideas may be explored in both absolute-drawings and completed buildings. This dual exploration is pointed out by Colin Rowe and Robert Slutzky in their essay, 'Phenomenal Transparency', where they attempt to show how the concept has been used in both building and drawing.[1] Although examples such as Robert Delaunay's *Simultaneous Windows* (1911) and Juan Gris' *Still Life* (1912) are compared in this essay, the drawings of Le Corbusier's *League of Nations Project* are compared to the constructed examples of the *Bauhaus, at Dessau* by Walter Gropius (1925-26). They are therefore comparing absolute-drawing examples in the first instance, but in the latter, they compare an interim-drawing example to a completed building. However, it is certain that when Rowe and Slutzky use the drawings of the *League of Nations Project* as examples, they are not using the drawings themselves but are interpreting them into what they think the building would be, as it is only through this interpretation that the idea of 'Phenomenal Transparency' may be perceived.

In conclusion, this interpretation of drawings, or any other creative medium, by looking more at its purpose than its form, gives a new possibility of understanding the creative output of either the artist or the architect. If we return to the three examples of the Santa Maria della Salute given at the beginning, the Corot painting is, hence, a first hand representation of ideas within the medium of drawing – an absolute-drawing; the plans of the Salute are second hand, two-dimensional representations of the ideas of the architect and therefore interim-drawings; and the completed building being a first hand representation (in three-dimensions) of those same ideas, making it an 'absolute-object'.

Notes

1 Rowe, Colin and Robert Slutzky, 'Transparency: Literal and Phenomenal', 1955-56; Colin Rowe, *The Mathematics of the Ideal Villa and Other Essays*, MIT Press, 1976.

FROM ABOVE: Langdon Cliffs Visitor Centre, Dover Harbour; Centre Régional de la Musique et de la Voix, Paris; Downpour, British Embassy, Oman

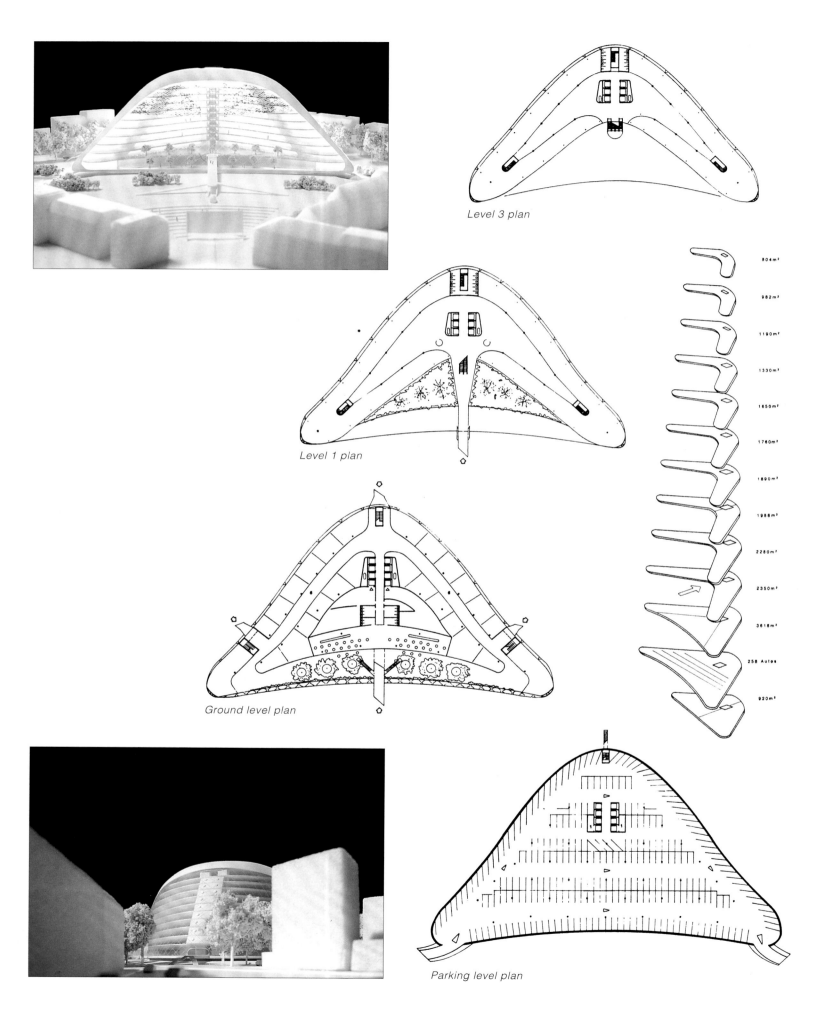

Level 3 plan

Level 1 plan

Ground level plan

Parking level plan

804 m²

982 m²

1190 m²

1330 m²

1650 m²

1760 m²

1890 m²

1988 m²

2280 m²

2350 m²

3618 m²

258 Autos

920 m²

FUTURE SYSTEMS
UMWELT HAMBURG

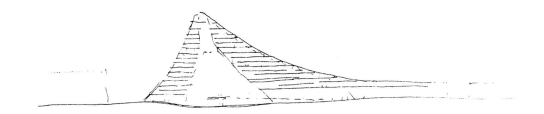

Set in 1992, the brief for this new 40,000m² headquarters for the city of Hamburg's environmental administration stated that the building must point to the future in terms of its energy consumption both during construction and in use in order to achieve an energy target of 50kN/m² per annum. The proposed site is in Altona, a relatively run down district of Hamburg, lying on a direct axis with the River Elbe.

As Hamburg is not only one of Europe's biggest ports but also a state in its own right and therefore of central importance to the New United Germany, the philosophy of the architects has been to reinforce Hamburg's pivotal position by proposing an architectural landmark and a radical approach to urban planning. Altona has a very strong connection to the river – a continuous green finger of the city stretching southwards to the Elbe. This connection, extending the linear approach to the building with the creation of two parks, has been emphasised by the architects so that the Umwelt gives back to the city an area of public space.

The building is clad in transparent glass and is shaped to minimise its surface area and maximise thermal efficiency. It is almost entirely heated and cooled by ambient energy sources.

The building form resembles an open leaf picked up at its centre and suspended from an inclined boomerang-shaped arch. A fine transparent net of glass is stretched over the structure to create a 'glass dune'. The softness of this aerodynamic form creates a calm environment in the surrounding areas, avoiding the turbulence created by more hard-edged structures. In the perspective of the curved planes, the height of the building disappears, minimising the impact of its scale and volume on the site.

The heart of the building is the atrium, a dramatic south-facing space, animated by the movement of escalators, by the changing light from the stained glass screen and by the motion of people within. Suspended in front of the atrium membrane is a stained-glass screen designed by Brian Clarke, a delicate mosaic of hovering colour following the curved plane of the transparent facade. As the sun plays on the crystal facade it catches the light of the screen, throwing shafts of coloured light in a soft dappled pattern on to the atrium floor. At night when lit from inside the structure will glow with a vibrating ultramarine, like an ocean-going liner at night.

All floors open out on to the atrium space thus ensuring clear orientation for both occupants and visitors. The naturally-lit circulation zones are generously planned to allow for reception, seating and coffee areas at each level which can also be used for informal meetings. This use of space enables the circulation area to become a dynamic part of the office environment and eradicates long dark corridors. Interdepartmental circulation is via escalators and, in addition, all floors are served by lifts. A public level with shopping arcades, a restaurant and a terrace overlooking the parks is accessed either from ramps around the park or directly from the Umwelt.

The key structural element of this project, developed in conjunction with engineers YRM Anthony Hunt Associates, is the inclined-boomerang shaped arch, a three-dimensional steel-clad prismatic truss spanning from ground level to the apex of the arch at the top of the central lift core. Suspended from the boomerang structure are the perimeter floor sections, while a single-glazed primary steel cable net forms the sealed outer skin of the building. This net is stabilised by strut connections against the floors. The floors are formed from hollow steel units supported on a grid of steel columns. The floor units are water filled to provide energy free mass, thermal capacity and fire protection.

The project's environmental strategy is based on a low entropy concept in which fresh cool air is drawn into the building at the base of the atrium and hot stale air exhausts through the louvres at roof level. An entirely glazed, sealed outer skin and an inner skin of openable glass louvres enables the air trapped between to be heated by solar radiation. Air movement is created by the buoyancy of warm air and rises due to the stack effect. The aerodynamic profile of the structure helps reinforce natural air-flow patterns within the building. Air flowing over the top of the streamlined atrium creates a zone of negative pressure which helps pull hot stale air out of the building

The architects' overall philosophy in the design has been to create dynamic interaction between the external weather conditions and the building itself, rather than opposing the climate with energy. The atrium volume and the double skin around the offices provide a thermal buffer to the building. It is this inner skin of openable glass louvres and retractable blinds that is adjusted according to season for comfort conditions. Light reflectors within the inner skin ensure natural daylighting during most of the year.

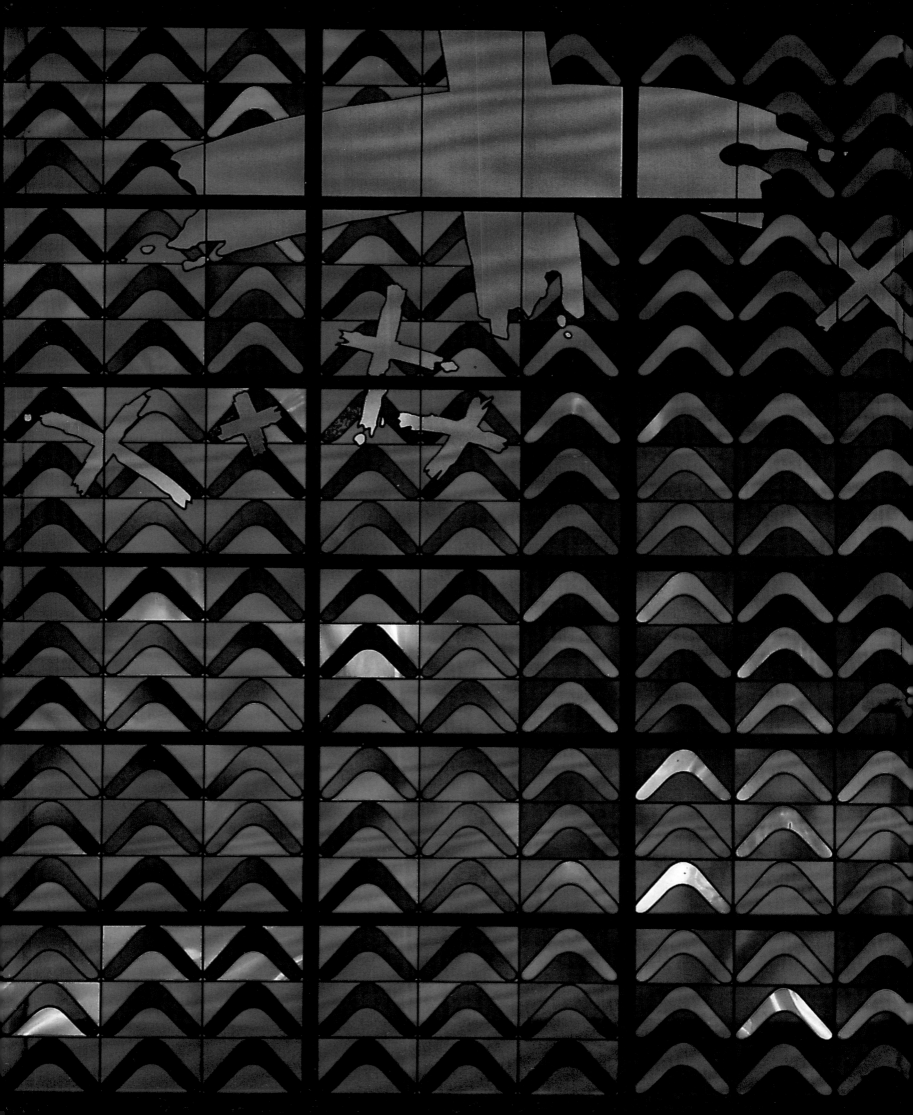

BRIAN CLARKE
STAINED-GLASS SCREEN FOR UMWELT HAMBURG

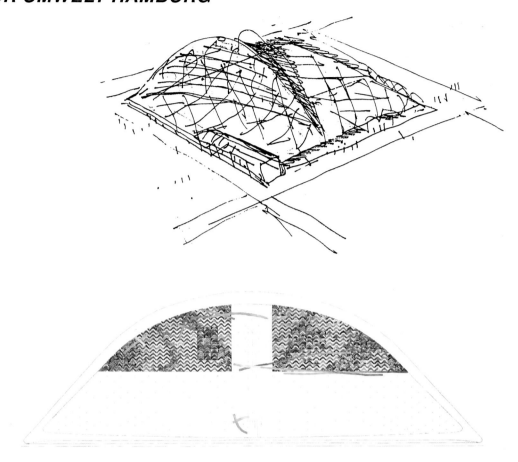

The forms created by Future Systems with their particular blend of organic Modernism provoked an altogether different approach from Brian Clarke.

Working from the so-called 'boomerang' plan of the building, Clarke constructed an internal 'skin of art' that spans the internal plane of glazing – an area of more than 1,100m². He felt that the bank of escalators climbing through the offices was an important 'animation' when viewed from outside, and that the view through the wall of glass was significant to visitors as they used the stairs when entering the building. Accordingly, he left the central area entirely clear except for two great ribbons of orange and yellow that dart across the space forming a bridge between the building halves and, lower down, skirting the entrance, and teasing the public in.

The atrial heart of the building would therefore become a dramatic south-facing space enlivened by the movement of people horizontally and vertically, and by the passage of light through the complex and delicate skin of colour. All the floors open directly on to this animated, light-filled atrium which also contains shops, restaurants and a terrace.

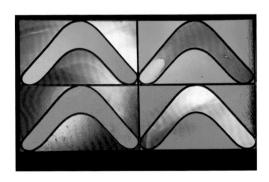

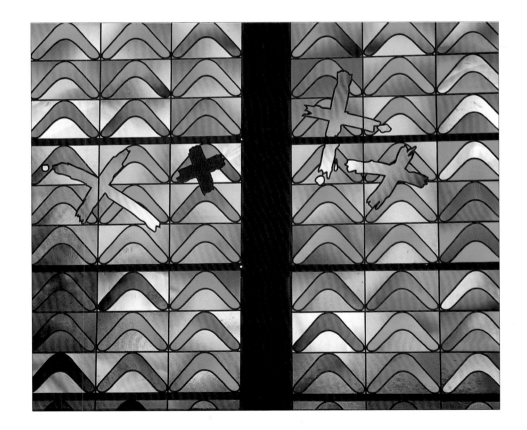

JOHN LYALL ARCHITECTS
TOTTENHAM HALE STATION FORECOURT

Commissioned by Haringey Council, this scheme is currently on site and continues John Lyall Architects' redesign of the transport interchange at Tottenham Hale, North London. Having already created the new railway station and having transformed the underground station, the practice has now developed a proposal to improve the forecourt area where passengers wait for buses and taxis. The scheme is also a continuation of the collaboration between John Lyall and the artist Bruce McLean.

New glass canopies and lighting are employed to create a safer, more direct pedestrian access to the station across the gyratory road system. The central island is brought to life by a linear fountain enclosed by a glass box beam beneath which people can walk (13.5 metres long and 6 metres high). It displays the passing of time by releasing a jet of water at fifteen-minute intervals. This is complemented by a tall, thin landmark beacon divided into twelve blue segments which light up gradually to mark every hour.

The public, waiting for buses or queuing in their cars at the traffic lights, is treated to a performance every quarter of an hour. On the hour all four water jets spring into action.

By studying both the beacon and the fountain, it is possible to tell the time. The fountain box also contains coloured glass, images, letters and numerals, all of which are animated by the play of water and light.

The team is working with local primary school children to generate stories and images which will be incorporated into the design by Bruce McLean. A selection of the children's words will be cast in terrazzo and set into a 50-metre length of paving across the site.

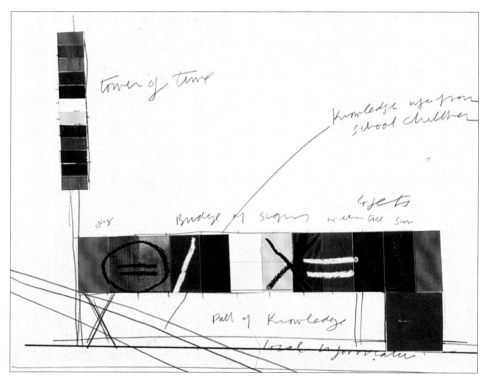

Tottenham Hale Forecourt, Bruce McLean conceptual sketch, mixed media

Tottenham Hale model photograph

THE ART SQUARE
Barnsley

A team consisting of John Lyall Architects, the artist Bruce McLean and the planner John Montgomery of Urban Cultures was commissioned in November 1996 by Barnsley Metropolitan Borough Council to produce a strategic proposal for employing art and culture to act as a catalyst for the regeneration of the centre of the town.

The proposal addresses an area of approximately 4 acres (125 x 125 metres) in which an 'art square' is established, creating a place in the centre of Barnsley where the commercial and civic environment is to be transformed and reactivated by the presence of art and the design of the space and its edges. The square is defined by Dog Lane to the west, Peel Square to the south, Market Hill to the east and Shambles Street and the Town Hall to the north.

It is delineated by either a line of lights or a glass-covered, back-lit trench and a line of paving. Within this initial framework or 'infrastructure' the Art Square would be curated like a gallery. Selected artists would be allocated a plot to work on, with the selection of artists involved changing over time, with some transformations or installations lasting longer than others.

The square would act as a new destination for leisure, retail and cultural activities, where people can either become involved in the activities or simply 'hang-out' and watch. It would also heighten the profile of Barnsley by identifying it with current activity in contemporary art, giving the city a national – or even international – name. In addition, the development would work as a catalyst for new commercial activity in this part of the town.

In planning terms, the scheme would act to reorganise traffic, parking and open spaces in the town to create a safer environment, transforming 'backland' areas and alleyways into pleasant places. It would also integrate the Town Hall and Library into the town centre.

As a 'notice board' for the town and as a place where its history could be depicted, the Art Square would belong to the entire population of Barnsley, which would have a role in directing the future development of the square.

The square is made up of a series of spaces defined as follows:

Town Hall Square

This area is currently used for surface car parking and traffic routes. It is bounded by tough-looking buildings, and incorporates a dramatic slope from west to east. The proposal would pedestrianise the area in front of the library to unite it with the square. The library building itself is somewhat hostile in appearance with its main entrance tucked away at the side. The architects propose to 'lighten' the

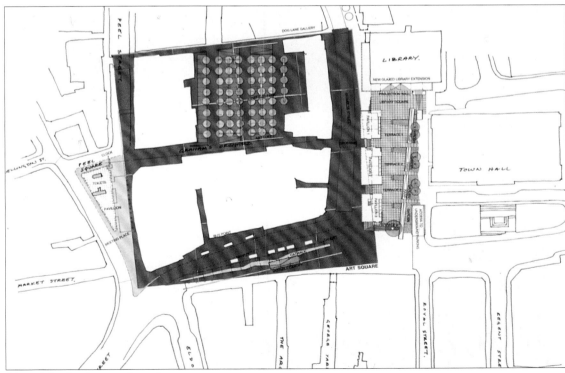

Plan of the Art Square, Barnsley

appearance of the south and east elevations by attaching a large glazed atrium, thereby reorganising the main entrance to face the square. In this way the library would be more welcoming, with its café and seating areas visible from the outside. The atrium wall will also support a large screen at high level for the projection of information, films and art pieces, which could be viewed from the new square, and which would also be visible from the bottom of Church Street and Market Hill.

From the library the square steps down in three distinct terraces each housing a simple, glass pavilion with darker and more solid accommodation at ground floor level. The pavilions would be used as temporary or permanent art galleries, as venues for music, receptions and shows, and for cafés and bars which would spill out on to the terraces. The changes in level would enable the incorporation of parking facilities beneath the terraces, which would be approached from the lowest point in Church Street. To ensure an appropriate quality of paving, planting and street furniture the architects would work in collaboration with artists.

Dog Lane and Grahams' Orchard

These streets are important historic links between Peel Square and Shambles Street. A committee of artists would be asked to make proposals to transform this area without removing either public car parking or servicing to the back of premises. For example, Grahams' Orchard car park could be re-terraced and laid out as an orchard with trees set out on a car parking grid. Or the car park itself could become a kinetic sculpture with cars, from time to time, being parked by colour to create abstract patterns. Pedestrian routes would be given equal attention, taking the narrow views and sloping topography into account.

Town Hall Square, Barnsley

Installations to Market Hill, Barnsley

Peel Square

Although not all the facades of the historic square at the end of Peel Street are praiseworthy, the square has a good spatial feel and is a natural place for people to meet.

The emphasis of the development would be on information, history, glass and time, celebrating the heroes of Barnsley and its industrial past (the glass industry and clock-making). An inventive town clock could be created as part of the pavilion, providing an opportunity to build high.

In this way, Peel Square would become a meeting place, a place for public speaking, for publicising events, and for sitting outdoors in good weather.

Market Hill

The 'market' quality of this stretch of road would be reintroduced with attractive, purpose-designed stalls selling produce. Existing car parking would be taken out, with only a one-way route for buses remaining, therefore allowing more space for pedestrians.

The 'strip' is defined by a long catwalk with a canopy which can be moved to a variety of locations. The catwalk design incorporates a framework with fixed canopies for market stalls on the southern side. It would be used regularly for either fashion shows or performance events. Areas adjacent to the catwalk would be designed by various artists.

Beyond the Art Square

A new landscaping is envisaged for Shambles Street, west of the library, with a line of trees and an improved environment for pedestrians in front of the zigzag block. New art and design-related workshops, galleries and businesses could be housed here.

Towards the east, the Art Square would act as a catalyst for the regeneration of George Yard with shops, restaurants and small businesses in converted premises.

The Art Square, Bruce McLean conceptual sketch, mixed media

The Art Square, Bruce McLean conceptual sketch, mixed media

BAUMAN LYONS ARCHITECTS WITH BRUCE MCLEAN AND MEL GOODING

REGENERATION OF SOUTH PROMENADE
Bridlington

Irena Bauman believes that for anyone who has witnessed the magic of the Trevi Fountain in Rome, the current debate about the relationship between architecture and art can seem regressive – especially as the latest revival of interest is driven by 'brokers' (art agencies) and by financiers (the Arts Lottery), and not by the practitioners themselves. Despite this, she believes a number of artists and architects have embraced the possibilities offered by collaboration, and as a result some thoughtful work is beginning to emerge.

Bauman proposes that there has always been a clear distinction between art and architecture for the simple but significant reason that the former fulfils physical function for the recipient – the user – whereas the latter provokes emotional response from the recipient – the audience. The relationship between product and beneficiary is therefore fundamentally different.

There are also, she believes, significant differences in the process of procurement.

Architecture is always site-specific, it is procured by a collaborative team of experts, and designing is separated from making. The creative elements are subordinated to various regulations, to specific programmes and budgets. In addition, clients tastes are frequently imposed upon the design team.

Procurement of art, however, seldom follows this route. It is more likely to be the product of one mind, conceived and made by the same person. Regulations, if relevant, are less critical, and clients generally have a high regard for the integrity of the artist and therefore refrain from influencing their work.

Bauman argues that these differences lead to serious difficulties with integrating the two disciplines, but that most collaborations bypass such difficulties by adopting a 'bowl of fruit' approach where members of the team each create their own elements which are then placed together, retaining individual integrity like pieces of fruit in a bowl – in effect an exercise in curation.

More challenging is what she identifies as the 'mixed fruit salad' approach where, as at Bridlington Promenade, architect and artist work together from the outset, achieving full integration in both process and production. The end product, if the collaboration succeeds, is a cohesively-designed element in which individual contributions remain distinct, like the pieces of a fruit salad, but which has an overall identity.

Irena Bauman, the architect, and Bruce McLean, the artist, established their response to the site, with its neglected mile-long promenade, over several visits and after intense discussion. The overwhelming impression of the site was of the dominating presence of natural elements – sea, sand, sun, sky, clouds and wind.

They quickly reached a consensus to explore repetition and rhythm in a controlled, man-made manner in order to contrast and therefore enhance the 'backdrop' of nature. They also agreed to build the design solution around natural resources, to explore opportunities

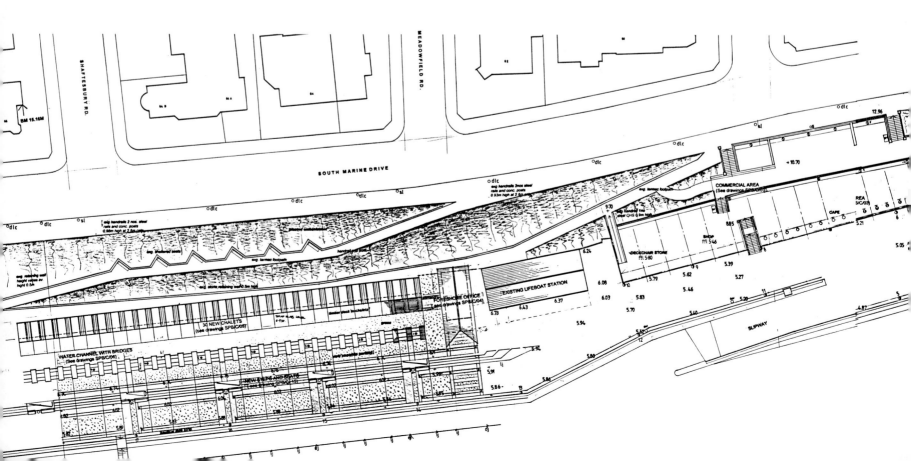

offered by constantly changing light, to harness wind to power the lighting, to insert architecture into landscape in such a way as to preserve the magnificent views of the sea, and to use materials in keeping with the location.

Site and brief were explored further in an intense three-day design session in which new preoccupations emerged – how to provide privacy within public space, and how to use colour.

Throughout the design period, differences in the working methods of the architect and the artist contributed to the creative process. The abstract paintings produced by the artist were constant interpretations of possibilities of form and materials explored by the architect.

The key elements of design emerged within the first four weeks of the collaboration. Chalets were separated from the promenade by a 200-metre-long water channel, with individual bridges linking each chalet to the space beyond and creating symbolic private space for each chalet user. A paddling pool with a face

feature made by the artist in terrazzo was incorporated. It was decided to power the sculptural shower walls with solar energy and to install a water wall at the south end of the channels which would establish a physical as well as a visual break between the two sections of the promenade. A mile-long text by Mel Gooding is spelt out in terrazzo along the full length of the promenade in a 600-millimetre-wide strip. It interprets the history of Bridlington and its natural resources, as well as documenting the experience of promenading and of the seaside. A steel jetty cantilevers from the edge of the promenade, and a café is built into the headland to explore the magnificent views of the sea. All these aspects of the project took form through a process of collaboration.

The result is art which has a physical function for the user and architecture which demands an emotional response from the audience – undoubtedly bridging the edge between architecture and art.

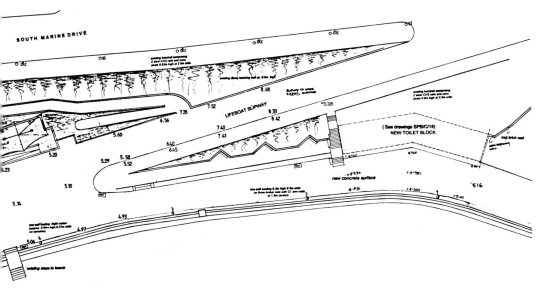

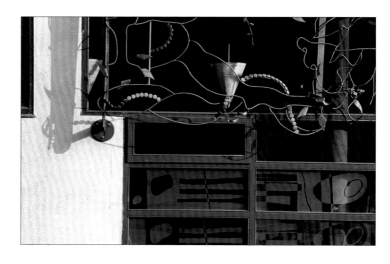

BAUMAN LYONS ARCHITECTS
LEEDS CHINESE COMMUNITY CENTRE

If architecture is an art form then architects are by definition artists. Once this is recognised, argues Simon Warren, project architect of this warehouse redevelopment in Leeds, there should be no theoretical barrier to other types of artist collaborating on buildings when the programme requires.

When artists from disciplines other than architecture are involved, Warren believes there is no limit to the range of collaborative work that can be undertaken. Either the visual artefact is not produced by the artist, but the encompassing direction and the theory of the project is or, at the other end of the scale, a visual artist creates an artefact that is integrated into the architecture.

This small scheme by Bauman Lyons Architects started out as the latter type of collaboration, with an artist creating an artefact. However, halfway through the project, circumstances changed and the architect ultimately took on the role of 'visual artist' as well.

The Leeds Chinese Community Centre is a four-storey, turn-of-the-century warehouse on the edge of the developing Chinese quarter near the centre of Leeds. It had been out of use for a number of years and was severely

dilapidated when purchased by the Leeds Chinese Community Association.

Most of the work involved essential structural repairs and weatherproofing, with only limited scope for innovation. However, the brief required that the new centre act as a visual focus to promote the activities of the Chinese community in Leeds. It was clear that the best means of achieving the required impact within a restricted budget was a new 'shop front' The facade was opened up to provide views in and out and increased daylight at ground floor level. A sculptural screen in metal designed by artist Madeleine Millar was inserted into this void at high level, with a secondary screen of etched glass to be placed behind it.

The brief for the screen was set by architect, client and artist, focusing on the narrative content of the design as well as its practical function – to protect the expanse of glazing behind it. Chinese cultural references are depicted in filigree-like metalwork which casts beautiful shadows into the building.

The sculpture combines found objects in steel with steel bars to form a Feng Shui-inspired composition of protective door gods. Bicycle chains are employed to great effect as moustaches for the

figures, and for the dragons which symbolise good fortune. A specially designed structural frame holds the sculpture in place.

Unfortunately, halfway through the project funding for the etched glass screen (which was to have been commissioned from another artist) was dropped. This led to the architect himself undertaking the work, armed with a £15 roll of sticky vinyl (a signage industry standard for mimicking the effect of etched glass).

Although the architect was initially somewhat uncomfortable about 'fooling' the public with the vinyl, he set out to explore the scope of the material. The vinyl was be cut out freehand with a scalpel blade, so sketches for a design were loose and amorphous abstractions.

The function of the 'etched' panel was to create a level of privacy for the centre users without restricting natural light. The design detail was ultimately shaped by consideration of patterns cast by shadows on to the floor, walls and columns of the space.

In the end the 'negative' of the design cut out for the lower panel was repeated in the upper panel, making the fullest use of the single sheet of vinyl and creating a dialogue between solid and void.

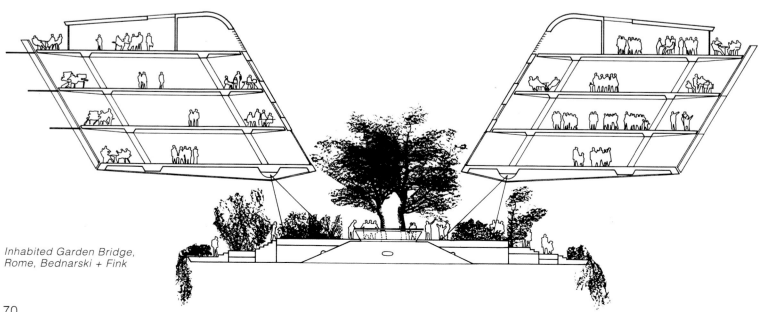

Inhabited Garden Bridge,
Rome, Bednarski + Fink

CEZARY M BEDNARSKI + PETER FINK
ART AND ARCHITECTURE

After two decades of active development of public arts in the UK very little progress seems to have been made in exploring the pivotal issues and rationale for collaboration between artists and others involved with the built environment. The discussion was, and is still, led by Public Art agencies and lobbies and does not seem to have developed beyond a series of general pronouncements on the desirability of such collaborations, and an advancement of mostly unsubstantiated socio-economic arguments, frequently used as a means to validate government led investment into the concept through either arts incentive awards or regeneration budgets. The emergence of lottery funding in this situation has considerably enforced the clear and strong economic self interests of the Public Art lobby and its motivation to promote artist/architect collaboration. The current understanding of the whole issue amounts to no more than restatement of the pragmatic adoption of culture since the Second World War by Western mass societies distinguished by a level of universal affluence as well as by a corresponding level of social stratification. Consequently, the discussion does not really touch on the underlying paradox of a society that feels comfortable with the idea of art and culture as an educationally instilled concept, but in practice is disinterested in the issue of critical legibility leaving culture to be dominated and driven by market forces. In turn this effectively condones the denigration of culture to a social engineering concept producing on one hand, an all pervading symbiosis of culture tourism and mass culture and on the other the extraction of 'high art' into the self validating and self serving art establishment. It is our belief that to be able to make any progress in exploring the issue of collaboration one must start from the examination of the actual personal practice and experiences of those engaged in collaboration. This is the first step towards an authentic and constructive understanding.

It is interesting to note that the discussion of the issue of collaboration seems to cause real difficulty all round, even though architecture was, and remains, a human activity highly dependent on team effort, not withstanding the individualist and lead role of the architect. Architecture is highly dependent on the active exchange of ideas, knowledge, skills and of labour. However the critical issue of who leads, when and how, and who dominantly shapes this process is not often discussed in any depth, as architects are accustomed to be nominally in charge. This notion is culturally endorsed by the emergence of the small percent of 'signature architects'. In the daily psychological reality of architecture as exemplified in the relationship between an engineer and an architect the question of who leads is never this clear.

Peter Rice in his book *Engineer Imagines* examines some of these issues by looking at what might be the difference between the engineer and the architect by saying that the architect's response is primarily creative, whereas the engineer's is essentially inventive.

The architect, like the artist, is motivated by personal considerations whereas the engineer is essentially seeking to transform the problem into one where essential properties of structure, material or some other impersonal element are being expressed. This distinction between creation and invention is the key to understanding the difference between the engineer and architect, and how they can both work on the same project but contribute in different ways. Indeed, now it is important that engineers start to educate both people within the profession and the public at large on the essential contribution that the engineer makes to even the most mundane projects.

He then concludes that the beginning of this process requires a full understanding of the problems faced by engineers as well as the examination of the position of the engineer in general.

In an interesting way this issue and some of the surrounding ambivalence can be currently detected in the relationships between architects, structural engineers and engineers specialising in large civil engineering projects such as bridge building. As bridges became the design icons of the nineties there is an intense revival of interest in exploring how architects could contribute to what was principally, until the arrival of Calatrava, the domain of a handful of niche civil engineering firms. It is interesting to note, in this context, the extent to which many engineers and architects in the UK are fundamentally critical of Calatrava's work in private, for example, frequently pointing to the extent to which its engineering clarity is, in their view, compromised by wilful architectural design. At the same time in public they pay lip service to his work as a 'positive' example of integration between engineering and architecture.

Ken Shuttleworth of Foster Associates in his talk 'Lipstick on a Gorilla' presented at the DHV conference on bridges tried to make a case for the inclusion of an architect in bridge building by saying:

> On a building, even a really big building, the architect is the king. On a bridge, even a really tiny bridge the engineer is the master and the architect chooses lamp posts. Why is this? Why is there a such a colossal difference in the way projects are organised? Why is it seen that there has to be a difference?

He then proceeds to make the case for architects to be included, by pointing out that:

> For me as an architect, the advantage of us working on the design of a bridge, is that we bring fresh approach. We encourage new thinking, challenge preconceptions and force engineers who have been designing bridges in the same way for years, to think again. More often than not an engineer will look at a solution for a bridge within a familiar and existing framework of ideas. Our advantage is that we don't bring any preconceptions to bridge design as we haven't done any before! This is our greatest strength.

It would be extremely interesting to see what the reaction would be if one substituted the notion of the bridge engineer for that of an architect, in an increasingly style orientated practice showing the first signs of design fatigue, and that of the architect with that of an artist. One could easily construct the dialogue around the example of the artist only being used by the architects in a patronising manner akin to specifying the lamp posts on a bridge. One could expect that this sort of argument about lack of practical experience being the greatest asset, if made by an artist, would not go down so well. Why then should bridge engineers be so enthusiastic to collaborate with architects on the basis of such an assumption?

In the light of this type of argument it is interesting to look at the engineers' reaction to the several bridges in existence or under construction in the UK where the design was architect led. In his article 'Should architects lead on bridge design?', Sydney Lenssen wrote: 'Don't be surprised to see the Department of Transport appointing an architect to design a major bridge sooner rather then later, leaving the architect to choose the engineer'. That would be taking matters too far for Ahm Povl of Ove Arup, who more fervently than most, led the crusade to improve British bridge design with the help of gifted architects. He said: 'But the danger is there and needs to be stopped.' Clearly if the engineer of his status is worried the issue at stake, i.e. of collaboration, warrants much more attention than it is receiving.

As a result of our collaboration on several bridge projects with both structural and bridge engineers we grew aware of these issues. Our experience of dealing with them became the catalyst for our exploration into the nature of the dialogue within the team and the need to deal directly and creatively with the issues of individual and mutual empowerment. As Peter Rice observed, the progress towards a concept of an expressed objective in the team design situation can be greatly influenced by the use of verbal communication and language as a key to what is happening. He observed that in his own experience in Britain sketching rather than talking is by far the more usual method of communication, a fact that he found constraining. In such an approach to architecture, the firming up of forms and the consistency of detailing assumes a value in itself. This in turn dramatically limits the opportunity to work collaboratively as it tends to exercise a deterministic control over such issues as intellectual basis, depth of meanings, external aesthetics and contextual urban design, all being project specific.

In the case of an artist and architect collaboration the key question is whether the artist is capable of making a contribution which opens a different perspective to architecture, or is this something to do with what the architects should be doing in the first place. Isamu Noguchi is one of the few artists working this century whose work made a coherent case for collaboration. In the fifties and sixties he worked with Gordon Bunschaft, the chief designer at Skidmore, Owings & Merrill and this still offers many useful pointers for today. They were introduced through Louis I Kahn, whose own thinking on architecture and art was profoundly akin to Noguchi's. As Kahn put it:

I only wish that the first really worthwhile discovery of science would be that it recognises that the unmemorable, you see, is what they are really fighting to understand, and the measurable is only a servant of the unmeasurable; that everything that man makes must be fundamentally unmeasurable . . . At the threshold, the crossing of silence

and light, lies the sanctuary of art, the only language of man. It is the treasure of shadows. Whatever is made of light casts a shadow; our work is of shadow; it belongs to light.

Around the same time Noguchi wrote: 'There is a difference between the actual cubic feet of space and the additional space the imagination supplies. One is measure, the other, awareness of the void of our existence in the passing world.' Kahn's reverence for light as a shaper of all things was, of course, particularly satisfying for a sculptor. When looking at the long and productive period of collaboration between Noguchi and Bunschaft it is important to note the extent to which Bunschaft as an architect consciously empowered the artist on one hand and on the other the extent to which the artist went in his desire to understand the concerns of the architect. Bunschaft was a firm believer in initiating the artist at the beginning of the project, so that his contribution became a functional part of the overall design, and it was his idea to have a sculptor to design the total space adjacent to a building as a means of humanising the ground level areas around it. Defining the physical limits of a project, serving as an interpreter of the client's needs, and projecting his own definite views, Bunschaft constantly urged Noguchi towards inventive solutions for these spaces.

The example of Noguchi illustrates another important aspect of the interrelationship between art and architecture. Throughout most of his life Noguchi in spite of numerous large scale projects around the world, was actively ignored by the art world considering him to be only a commercial artist. He even remarked that he was 'the successful, unsuccessful sculptor'. Only when it became apparent that trying to uncritically import gallery artist into architecture could lead to disappointments, did Noguchi's work start to be seen for the achievement it represents.

In the UK we can now see the same process at work producing many local projects equivalent to Richard Serra's arc for New York, such as the now defunct Ash and Silk glass box by Vong Phaophanit in Greenwich. In this instance a Public Art Agency involved a gallery artist who produced a major work out of glass for an urban park in an industrial neighbourhood of London. This wholly inappropriate response to a site led not to a removal of the work as in the case of Serra but to its damage through vandalism. Whilst many participants in this project were doubtful about the direction it was taking, they were swept aside by arguments about aesthetics and the need not to compromise the artistic vision. The role of aesthetics is particularly interesting in relation to collaboration between architects and artist, and in relation to the public perception of the personal aesthetic iconography. The personal is of lesser interest, what matters is the shared.

Peter Brooks, the theatre director, in an interview recently touched on one of the fundamental dimensions of collaboration when he said: 'For the person who is touched by the transcendental nature of human experience, the WHY forgets the HOW. On the other hand, everyone who is acclaimed as a good craftsman and a real professional carries the danger that through their craftsmanship, their professionalism, their routine, the great WHY shrinks to the proportion of HOW'. Comparing the rhythm of a game of football with a theatre play Brook says: 'Within playing, lightness, seriousness, all fall into place as the movement of the ball which is sometimes quick and sometimes slow and sometimes stops for a moment.' There is no preconception or control behind the rhythm of a football match. Yet the natural rhythm and excitement is always there.

As can be seen from our joint work our current position has

evolved from a shared and firm belief that the times of an architect 'architecting', an engineer 'engineering' and an artist 'decorating' are over, and that the issues facing architecture and art are best tackled in 'the natural rhythm of the football match'. Undoubtedly this does require in the first instance a mutual will to play on the same team and a trust in the abilities of your fellow players. Many artists at the moment, similarly to many architects, do not seem to realise that this involves a conscious decision to prepare yourself and to make an effort to understand each others' method of working and concerns. It requires a conscious decision to leave your 'usual hat' behind and open yourself to the unknown world of a new project. It seems to us that various issues such as using information and emotions as building materials in architecture, the exploration of the cultural and contextual limits of materials, interactivity and mutability of object architecture, the sustainability beyond the environmental, to mention just a few, could benefit from a process of investigation involving a broader collaborative base, where an artist could have a valuable contribution to make.

We share in the belief that the childish fascination with our newly acquired ability to force technology to do anything we can think of, so evident in the late twentieth century, will subside in the next Millennium. It will give way to an intelligent and creative search for more reasoned, deeper felt solutions to our architectural needs. We consider that none of the well established and, indeed, already worn out, bridge design idioms and stylistics will be of interest. No 'Calatravesque' or other stylistics. In fact no style at all. As Balanchin used to say 'refining all possibilities to one that is inevitable, simple and clear' is the way forward.

> Genuine courage requires facing reality, facing accelerating change in a world that has no automatic brakes. This poses intellectual, moral and political challenges of great substance [. . .] Our machines are evolving faster than we. Unless we learn to live with them safely, our future will likely be both exciting as well as short.

This statement by Eric Drexler sets out explicitly our concerns as well as setting out a 'playing field' for our collaboration.

Albert Dock Bridge, Liverpool, Bednarski + Fink

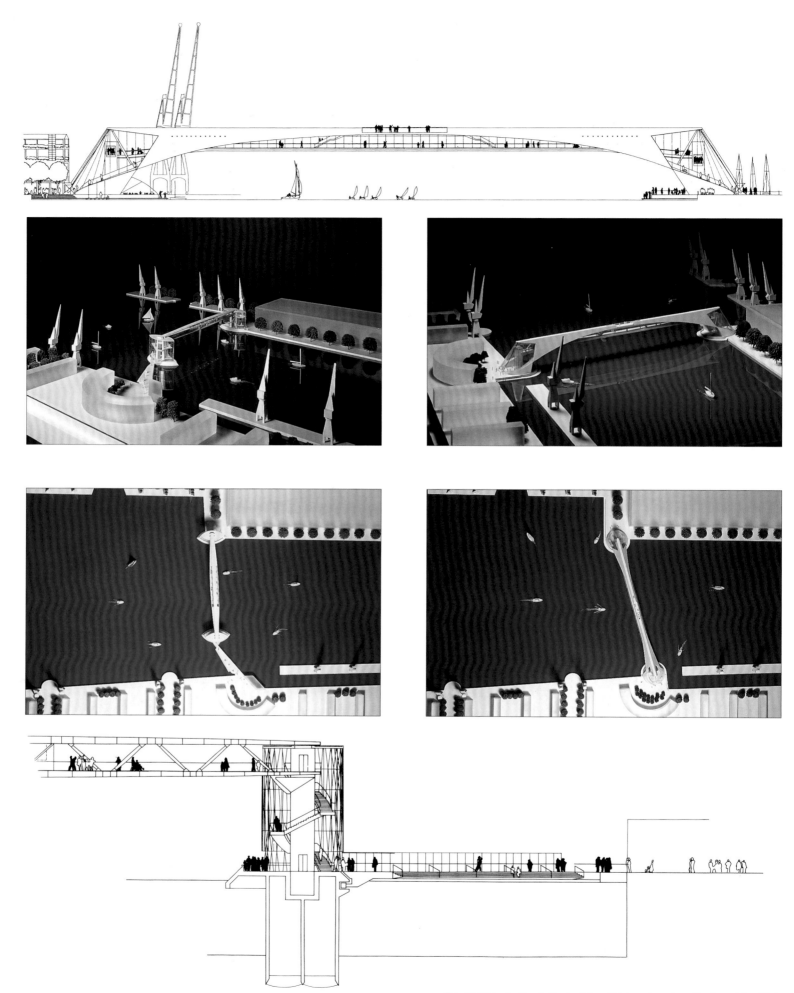

Royal Victoria Dock Pedestrian Bridge, London, Bednarski + Fink

THE ROYAL VICTORIA DOCK PEDESTRIAN BRIDGE
London

The brief of the limited competition in which these designs were finalists asked for an openable and a fixed bridge and the best possible design in terms of aesthetics, function and economics. We therefore proposed two designs stemming from the same philosophy. Both offered excitement – the fixed bridge through the use of steel plate construction which led to a striking form; the openable one through a novel design using a truss beam in which the diagonals are partially located on the centre line and partially on the edge lines of the deck. Besides rudimentary enclosed pedestrian links, there is no UK precedent for enclosed bridges. The fixed bridge designs represent our search for such a design idiom.

The involvement of an artist in the collaborative design process was seen as an opportunity to positively influence the provision of the spaces contained in the bridge as well as the appearance of the structure itself.

Lighting formed an integral part of the design of the bridge. The structures of both bridges represents an opportunity for an imaginative lighting scheme to transform the bridge into a powerful horizontal counterpoint to the illuminated pyramid of Canary Wharf Tower, as well as turning it into a celebratory landmark.

The detailed design will develop the possibility of colour washes of the main surfaces of the cantilevered sections, with emphasis given to the illumination of the underside of the pedestrian dock, creating a connecting ribbon of light as well as a clear reflection in the water.

Fixed Bridge

We considered it imperative to safeguard the Royal Victoria Dock as a sailing facility while making the crossing of the dock a pleasurable, uplifting and safe civic experience. The choice of steel plate was dictated by both structural and aesthetic considerations. Plate technology has been traditionally the building method of the shipping industry. A strong horizontal form with a proportion of its walls in solid plate would attract light during the day and be a rewarding object to light at night. The proposed bridge uses its structure as an element of environmental enclosure.

The bridge has been conceived as a series of spatial experiences. The arrival, dock-side spaces have a festive quality. The deck can be reached by one of two lifts, or by gently rising palatial stairs. Walking through the bridge one experiences a series of varying ambiences ranging from the brightness and openness of the glazed semi-conical canopy, through subdued transitory space with the 'muscular' cantilever build of the bridge evident, and on to the centre of the bridge span offering high opening and the best views. On the high level platform the ambience is similar to that of an open cockpit aeroplane, affording panoramic views with all of Docklands at one's feet.

Our intention was to design a place rather than a route. A place for people to go to rather than a passage to pass through. A place endowed with civic qualities similar to those of the Eiffel Tower.

With no clear brief as to the required relationship between the bridge and the dockside users, we opted for a self-sufficient, independent facility. On the south side the semi-cone of the entrance canopy makes the high point of the structure recede, reducing the perceptible mass of the form. It would thus not dominate the Peabody Crescent and on one side complement the exhibition centre.

Openable Bridge

Governed by the same design principles as the fixed bridge, the openable alternative crosses the dock in one single span. The potentially lopsided crossing has been mitigated by setting the fixed bridge deck at a right angle to the southern dock wall and by linking it by an openable deck to the required landing point within the Peabody Crescent.

In order to reduce the potentially overwhelming impact of the bridge access structure on the Peabody Crescent the openable deck is located at the southern end of the bridge at the same level as the dockside. With the south-west and north-east being the prevailing wind direction, the openable deck has a two-metre-high glass screen along its north-east facing edge. Broad steps down to the water level on this side of the deck face the south-west and are a welcome amenity for sitting out as well as being a landing facility for smaller boats.

An on-board reversible electric motor moves the openable bridge supported on an articulated joint on the dock-side. Its other end floats, being a monocoque shell structure, further aided by a buoyancy 'bladder'.

Access to the main bridge deck is through two support structures, each with two sets of stairs and two lifts. The large west and east facing landings serve also as viewing platforms towards Canary Wharf and City Airport. The main deck offers a weather protected space, while making it possible to walking the open air over almost half of the bridge. The central part of the bridge features open air areas shaded by 'pergolas' which will be used when crossing the bridge in good weather and as places of rest and contemplation. They are perfectly located for watching the sun rise and set over Canary Wharf and City Airport.

The stair/lift ends of the bridge are protected from inclement weather by glass skirts suspended from reinforced concrete roofs which in turn rest on cantilevers extending from the lift shafts. The skirts terminate 2.6 metres above deck/island level, leaving open viewing platforms for public gatherings and watching water events. The use of colour tinted glass, artwork and lighting effects have been envisaged for the skirts.

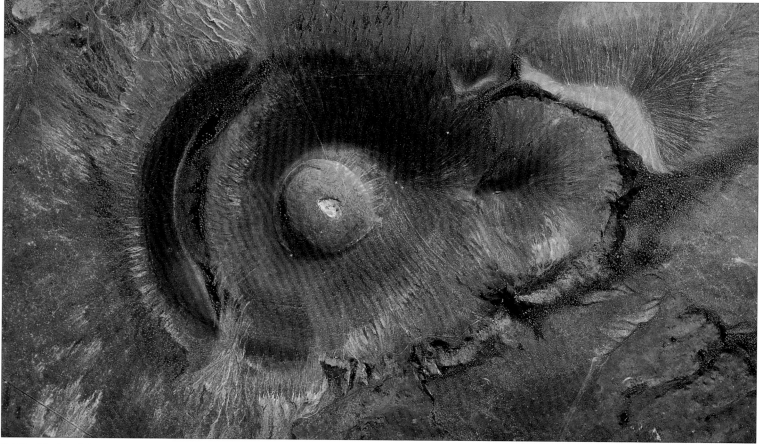

Roden Crater, Arizona

JAMES TURRELL
INTERVIEW BY ESA LAAKSONEN

Esa Laaksonen: I would like to discuss your views on light which is the main issue within your work, and the sensitivities of the human body to light and colour, and also your thoughts about perception. I understand that you have spent a long time in solitude, in prison and in darkness – therefore, it seems to me that the power of force in your work lies within the experiences that you had in asylum. Is that correct?

James Turrell: It was certainly formative in a sense that these experiences formed the will to work with light. In terms of being an artist I can't say that I took that experience well, because it was forced upon me – nor did I systematically explore what it is to have that aloneness, that solitary quality, without being forced into it. Now, with will and with free choice, I enjoy it.

The question about light. First of all, I would like to say that there is never no light – the same way you can go into an anechoic chamber that takes away all sound and you find that there never really is silence because you hear yourself. With light it is much the same way – we have that contact to the light within, a contact that we often forget about until we have a lucid dream. Asking ourselves where the light in the lucid dream comes from gets us near to these thoughts about the power of light. This power has, first of all, power in its physical presence. I like to bring light to the place that is much like that in the dream – where you feel it to be something itself, not something with which you illuminate other things, but a celebration of the thingness of light, the material presence, the revelation of light itself. This is something that allows light to live more than the forming of it. A lot of the learning to work with light, since it doesn't form by working with the hands as clay does, is this working with light through thought. There is an architecture of thought, the structuring of logic, of thinking, of the space of thought, and that is the province of architecture as much as building these buildings that we work in and use in a very pragmatic sense. Music structures this as well, as do certain things in art.

At this moment, I'm working very primitively with light, because I don't have many instruments with which to work it, but I work it in the way I can, and that is mainly to bring to the conscious awake-state, the light that inhabits these spaces that we know in the dream. So it's not a surprise for anyone to see the light like this, but it is a mild surprise to see it here because it seems to have this other quality, slightly other-worldly in that we know it from another place but we do not know about it. In architecture we discuss the space between form and it being positive and being filled. But rarely do we create this space. It's more rhetorical. So that when you see it, it is not a surprise.

EL: This brings us to the idea about entering a space, the entrance, airports and coming.

JT: Submission and the idea of what it takes to enter the space of a book. When we open a book and read it, often people pass through the space where we are reading and we are so in the space of the book that we don't notice people passing by and in a sense we are more in the book, in a space generated by the author, than we are in the physical space where we physically sit. This price of admission that was paid by submitting and giving over to the book, is also something that is required in terms of looking at architecture and entering a building, entering a space with that kind of quality, as well as is in looking *into* a work of art as opposed to looking *at* it. Looking at it is something that's very difficult. You see this in how people react to contemporary art, because there is some reason why they have difficulty deciding to enter it

So that's the price of admission. That we've made the price high, maybe a bit too high, is something art needs to think about, architecture as well. But we've made it high because it has taken a lot to do this and I guess that's a part of the reason. In terms of spaces, spaces before the space, spaces before the work, you have this pre-loading in the way of setting someone up for the experience to come – whether its just with dark adaptation, the time to let the eye open, or whether it is a loading with a certain colour so that when they come into another colour, this mixing of after image and colour from the image happens and enriches the experience. There's a lot of this that does go on in making these spaces.

EL: So you are also talking about concentrating and giving time and allowing time for perception when entering.

JT: Yes, this entry is very important, because, first of all, in time given there is grace. This mercy asked for is actually time. Time to change your life as in asking God for mercy, it's like asking for more time to change, to alter, whatever. But in terms of an experience, that grace is to give it time so that it does not have to be an impact piece that is seen and beheld with one glance. I want something to grow on us. So that it begins to realise itself slowly, not all at once.

EL: It is like entering an old cathedral in relative darkness and giving yourself time to adjust to the peace and the light and the interior colours.

JT: Your colour sensitivity will open up, your eyes open up to themselves. By giving it time there is discovery. It is sort of sublime and this is part of it for me, this something that doesn't happen at once: this revelation that isn't given all at once. It's a bit like the difference between sportive lovemaking and then actually making love with someone you love, its quite a different situation.

EL: At the moment you are building this huge project in Arizona in Roden Crater and I find the architecture that you are building

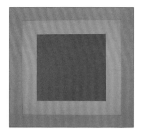

Skyspace I *(day), 1972*

Skyspace I *(twilight), 1972*

there really special. Actually, you are not really building space but you are building instruments for light.

JT: Generally I would say that I make these spaces to capture and hold light. So I must use form, but I'm really involved in making architectural space. For me the form must become secondary. It's nice to have a volcano because that's going to be the form and that's not something I made. But it allows me to have many curvilinear spaces that are neutral. If I have a rectilinear space, as we have in this room and most rooms for the exhibition of art, and if I can make an elliptical space in those rectilinear rooms, it's very strong because it is no longer neutral in the rectilinear building. But our vision is not rectilinear, our vision is sort of two spheres together that actually make an ellipsoidal shaping of the perceptual field.

So if you create spaces that are rectilinear and still have them neutral in this very curvilinear, voluptuous earth form of the volcano in which all the forms are actually parabolic or elliptical ... There's one circular part, one crater that is actually within seven feet of being circular on a radius of 800 feet, 814 feet. It is within seven feet of being a perfect circle, which is amazing. This gives me a way to make curvilinear spaces neutral, whereas it is not quite as appropriate in museums and spaces that are rectilinear. The rectangle, sort of the slightly off square is much more neutral than is a circle or an ellipse in these situations. Otherwise it can become shaped canvases. When you come in you can see that there is forming of form, but what becomes very positive is this thing between the space, in the work that I do. At the crater I make an architecture of space and I use these forms to capture the light, to hold it, to, in a way, give it form, give it the space to reside. But its clear that its done so that it doesn't reside on the wall. The light seems to fill the space. I think that's something you can feel. But it needs this architecture of form as well to capture light. Because I don't want to take away from the form of the volcano, making everything underground avoids actually forming the outside of these spaces into a building. They are in fact built but they are underground so that the outside really continues to be the volcano. The reason that they are underground is partly for that fact, but more for the fact that I make light powerful by isolating it, and also that it is not very much light that I isolate. You may be looking at the light of Venus alone, if you are dark-adapted for about an hour and a half ... We see that well!

The reason I do this is that if you take your flash into a cave or a place that excludes all other light, it becomes quite powerful. So I need to have these spaces that are protected from other ambient light. I'm just taking the light from where I want it. So that's why there is this underground architecture that in a way shares its outside form and opening with the bunker as in bunker architecture. Where the openings are made precisely, everything else is protected. In that way it also gives protection, it's cool in

the summer and actually somewhat warm in the winter. You can have places that capture and hold heat by being contained at the top and will become cold sinks by letting hot air go out and yet are shaded. This gives me a way to have a kind of a sparkling elegance in the human inhabiting of these spaces but it's made primarily for the habitation of light. That is something we can walk through, even though all these sinks are completely open. That is, there is no glass: I can make the feeling of glass or the ending of the space quite easily, visually without having to do it with material. Everything is open, but at the same time it is protected, that's why it's underground.

This architecture, in terms of its forms, shares similarity with the bunker architecture, in terms of its openings, except that we're not looking at fields of fire, we are looking up to certain portions of the sky and protecting all else, and on the interior formed out in a way that it speaks of the naked eye observatory, say at Tycho Brahe or the work of the astronomer Jai Sing in Jaipur and Delhi. So it has that kind of design from the outside-in aspect and it does have an architecture of form which I utilise to capture the light and hold it, thereby making a certain architecture of space.

I also pay attention to looking out from a space as in PSI Gallery's 'Meeting' (1980-86, Long Island City, New York) so that there is not only accepting light in maybe deeper space and out of the space. So I'm trying to pay attention to those qualities and in doing that in the outside form – where architecture normally has its sense of style – I have nothing because that's just the volcano.

EL: Is Roden Crater your lifework?

JT: Well, a little bit that way. But on the other hand I'll have to get that done so that I can get on with my lifework. It's a project that is a little bit too big for me to bite off and chew easily. We'll be finished a little bit before the year 2000. But we decided to restore the natural site and that will take time and then we also need to prepare some other things in terms of access and in other things of this sort. That's a good time for us to begin.

EL: For me the life span of the happenings at the Roden Crater projects is enchanting.

JT: To some degree I made a pre-made ruin. I have to confess that I have a great love for civic space that is emptied of use. Which would be something like Monte Albán or Chitzen Itza or Delphi or Valley of the Kings. These are things that once had use. Now these are just open to the elements and you have to just feel what goes on there by the feelings that the spaces gives to you and you surrender to that experience. In a way I wouldn't mind seeing Washington DC emptied of use. It would be very bizarre. Here is this giant man sitting in this house: Abraham Lincoln, a

Afrum-Proto, *1967*

Raemar, *1968*

sort of bizarre human being in terms of his appearance. We have made huge reflecting pools and then little pavilions that almost turn into follies which is very interesting to me. I'm interested in making a space that has qualities we discover just from the space itself, not through any sort of use of other than some imagined use to them. That kind of space that you wander in and out of and through things is a space that I like very much.

I like the quality in permanence and impermanence. There are some airfields for World War II that the Americans used in the American desert to practice. Now they are being taken over by sands and by sage brush and also they are going under the ground. Ground is closing over them . . . But if you fly over you can just see the ghosting of this, even though it is completely covered with sand. Very thin at the moment, but its only 45-50 years now. The lines of Nazca form a very beautiful plan. Its like the earth is an emulsion that you are looking at. You see some things developing, coming out early in development and then some of these things can get covered by other things at later

stages of development. Also, there are some things that can be sort of blown away and then they start to come out. Old civilisations that begin to be exposed.

EL: I think somehow you are now touching the main qualities of art and architecture.

JT: Well, I hope so. I'm just one artist. You have just a view point in any work. It can't be everything to all people. You have some parts that you work on. I'm interested in those, time-sense, and that's one reason I use light. Even though light is passing through at 186 thousand miles per second, in fact there is a certain permanence to it, which is interesting . . .

This interview first appeared in ARK (Finnish Architectural Review), 5-6 1996. The conversation was held during the 'Permanence' Symposium at the Virginia Polytechnic Institute Department of Architecture, Blacksburg, Virginia, on 23 March 1996.

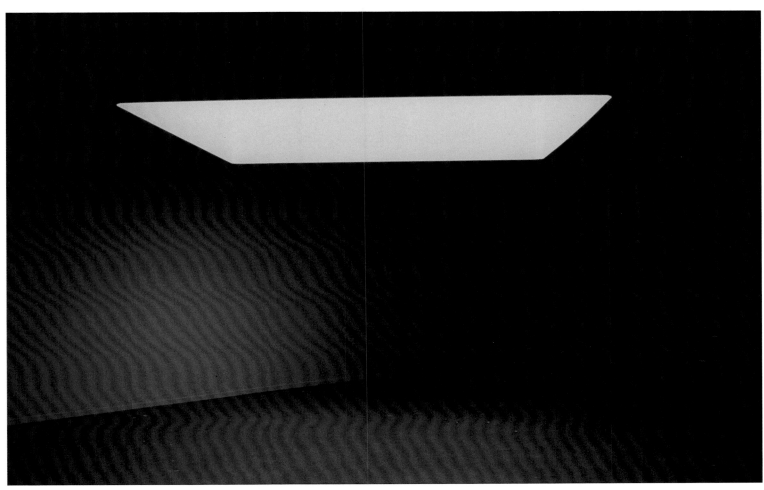

Hover, *1983*

JANE HARRISON AND DAVID TURNBULL

HYBRID
Utrechtsebaan Tower

The brief for this research project undertaken by Jane Harrison and David Turnbull in conjunction with Cecil Balmond and Nick McMahon of Ove Arup and Partners International was to study the potential construction of hybrid structures above the Utrechtsebaan urban motorway in The Hague.

A case study proposed a combination of hotel, restaurant, health club, bar, offices, café, and parking facilities in a single structure spanning the motorway and supported on either side by 1-metre-wide strips.

The solution is a generic enclosure with a stack of individually identified volumes inside which articulate the differences and overlaps between discreet programmatic zones. The enclosure has affiliations with other generic towers in The Hague, therefore establishing a large-scale pattern of relationships across the city. In this proposal the motorway is perceived as a significant 'earthwork' or land form, as well as being an essential and highly effective piece of infrastructure – a condition which should not be denied. This approach meant that the project stood separately from the 'romantic' schemes presented by other entrants such as Rob Krier, who proposed covering the motorway with gardens – apparently entirely curing the 'sickness' of the modern city.

FROM ABOVE: Field of generic towers, Utrechtsebaan; external envelope (partial mirror curtain wall) and internal envelope (timber and steel); plan sequence; OPPOSITE, L TO R: Sequence of axonometrics exploring pathways, programmatic and volumetric overlaps; coloured model interior, clear model interior; montage – 'maximum volume, minimum support'

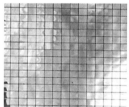

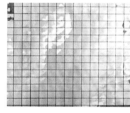

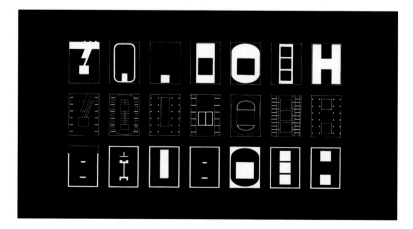

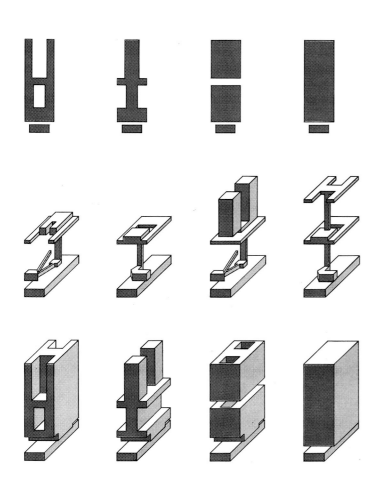

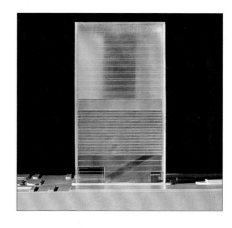

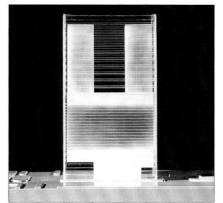

1.0　　　　　　2.0　　　　　　3.0　　　　　　4.0

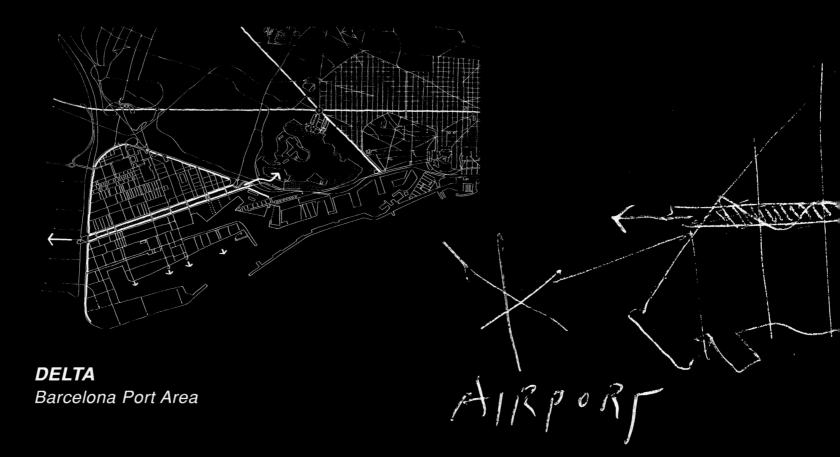

DELTA
Barcelona Port Area

Set by the Union Internationale d'Architecture (UIA) in 1996, the brief for this project required the definition of the access and service areas of the ZAL (Logistic Activity Zone) of the Port of Barcelona. The site is the River Llobregat delta, situated between coastal mountains and the sea, and separated from the historic centre of Barcelona by Montjuic Hill. As a geographical formation the delta plays a fundamental role in the region's economy, incorporating large expanses of irrigated land, tourist facilities, residential and industrial developments, fairgrounds, the airport, and the commercial and industrial port.

Harrison and Turnbull's project proposed that the scope of work established by the UIA competition brief for the access and service area should be reconsidered, and that the organisation of the port area and shoreline should be reappraised.

In their scheme a median band is defined between the shoreline condition of the port and the inland areas. This band is cleared and established as a wetland reserve (slow space). Roads on either side of the band are elevated to allow rapid transit from the airport to the city across the port (fast space). This allows the extension of the port area as a continuous grid with the efficiencies that this implies in terms of infrastructure and building shape, and avoiding the discontinuities between new and old areas suggested by existing plans for the port.

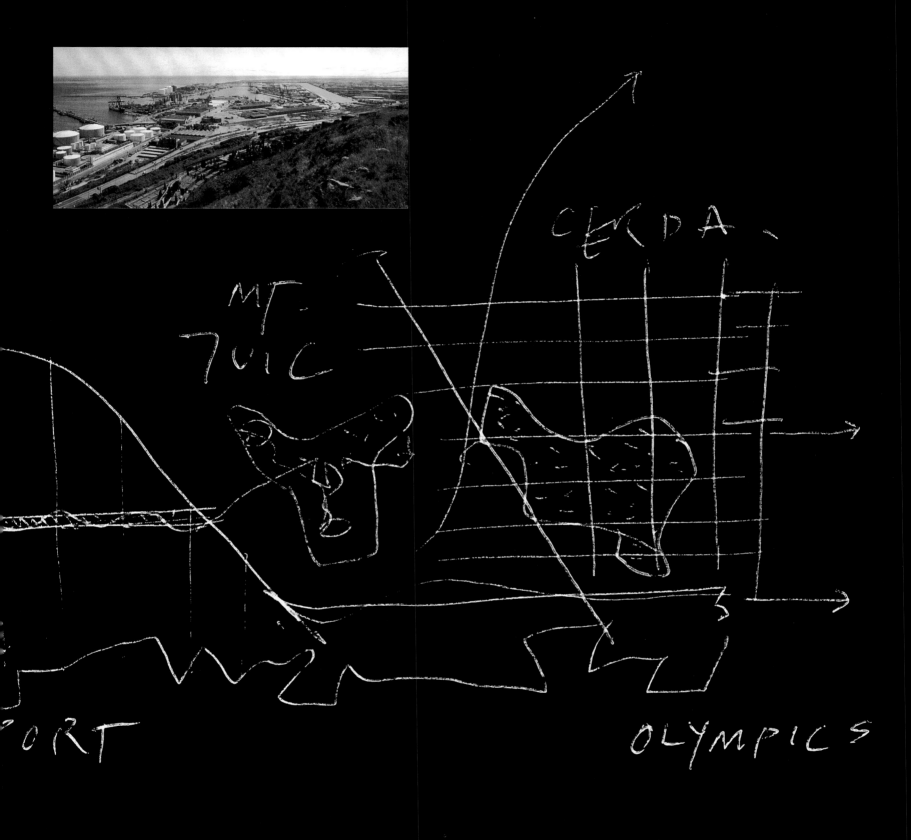

MT.
7VIC

CERDA

PORT

OLYMPICS

FROM ABOVE: Montage showing wetland strip
(slow space); Strategic connections;
OPPOSITE, FROM ABOVE: Four samples of
pre-existing floodplain conditions:
1.0 – woodland/grassland habitat;
2.0 – erosion control;
3.0 – stormwater filtration/treatment area;
4.0 – open water pond/storage;
BELOW: Plan of proposal

84

SAUERBRUCH HUTTON ARCHITECTS
CENTRE FOR INNOVATION IN PHOTONICS
Berlin

Due for completion in 1998, the two new buildings of the Photonics Centre in Wissenschaftsstandort Adlershof (a new business and science park for Berlin) accommodate laboratories, workshops, production facilities and offices for the client, WISTA GmbH. The buildings are conceived as soft-contoured volumes which create a strong identity within the existing rectilinear context and yet do not challenge the gentle coherence of the site. The sinuous forms of the buildings are at the same time a direct response to the requirements of the brief.

The minimal circulation requirements and the need for large zones without daylight (for optical laboratories) led to a deep plan in the main building. A central spine runs along the length of the building and lettable units, varying in size according to undulations in the plan, are laid out along it at right angles. The facade is double-skinned, enabling natural ventilation of offices at the perimeter whilst also providing a thermal buffer.

Services are integrated into the structure through vertical shafts located along the spine, from where they are distributed horizontally within the channels of U-shaped concrete beams, allowing all the services to reach every part of the building for maximum flexibility.

The smaller building provides a flexible 7.5-metre-high production space for large-scale experiments. It is conceived as a simple steel building with walls made entirely of glass.

The facade of each building appears to be clad in a varying spectrum of colour. This, combined with the undulations of the facades, leads to a building edge which is perceived as oscillating.

The double-skinned facade performs as a component of the natural ventilation system and is determined by the integration of the concrete columns within the facade itself. The paired columns are located within the depth of the facade to divide it into zones for the intake and extraction of air.

Incoming air is brought into the void of the double facade at each floor level via a slot in the outer skin and through sash windows on the inner skin. Each occupier can ventilate their office to individual requirements. Warmed outgoing air rises through holes in the columns into the stack, and escapes into the open air through louvres in the external skin at the topmost edge of the building.

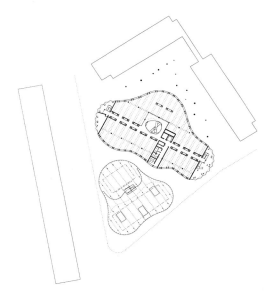

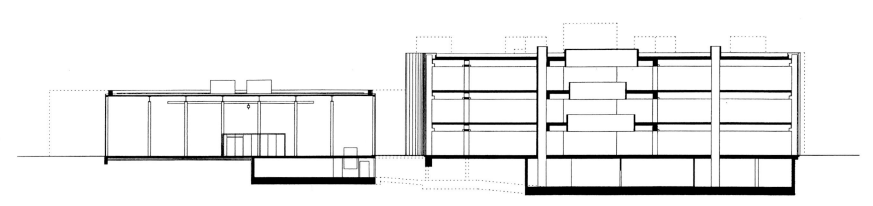

FROM ABOVE: Context; plan; section

RICHARD WENTWORTH
LITTLE DIFFERENCES
Christ Church Picture Gallery, Oxford

Richard Wentworth emerged as a new force in British art in the late 1970s. His sculpture creates unexpected alliances between familiar objects and evolves from an acute observation to the details of his surroundings. In 1996 Wentworth was commissioned by The Laboratory at the Ruskin School of Drawing and Fine Art to create a work which related specifically to the architectural surroundings of Christ Church Picture Gallery. The result was a show entitled 'Little Differences' created in collaboration with Jim Moyes.

Wentworth has said about this project: 'Christ Church Picture Gallery presented me with an overwhelming sensation of a collection in its bunker. The fact that the Powell and Moya building is indeed purpose-built is more than confirmed by the actual physics of the pictures in their container – the feeling that the buried building is filled to capacity with its pictorial contents, now retrieved from the old library home.'

'I have used the opportunity to exhibit . . . in two distinct ways. Firstly, I have separated two or three pictures and given them "pride of place", which is sufficient uninterrupted space to consider them exclusively and, by "calming" some of the walls, to point out some of the architectonic aspects of the place. Secondly, I have introduced into the space new works by myself and one by artist Jim Moyes. I have recently made various works using books, as much for their physicality as their content. By producing "kebabs" of differing lengths made of books, I have "sized up" the building, mimicking some of its details and measurements, lengths, heights and widths, much as cubits, rods and chains once did. Books are thereby used simultaneously to furnish and describe the interior . . The long shelf which accompanies the corridor is an internal datum of the ground level outdoors, a massively elongated threshold which reminds us of the spaces of cloisters and from which we view the lawn. Into this lawn, I have set a number of books cast in ferric gypsum, half-buried so that they appear to float in their host, the grass.'

FROM ABOVE: Making Do and Getting By, *1972;* Legend, *1996;*
OPPOSITE: Little Differences, *1996*

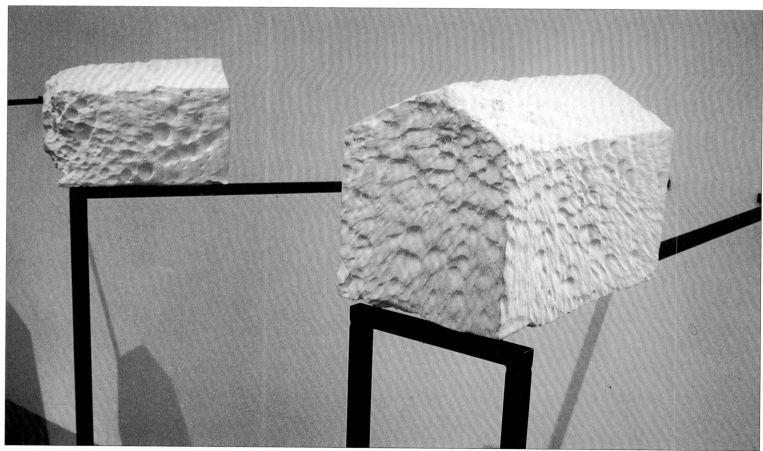

FROM ABOVE: General view of installation in the Long Gallery, Nuova Icona; close up of eroded plaster aedicules

PIERRE D'AVOINE WITH HEATHER ACKROYD AND DAN HARVEY

HOST

A Critique by Clare Melhuish

Venice is a city which has captivated the human imagination for centuries by virtue of its unique location, built on water, its close connection with the East through its command of the spice trade into Europe, and its wealth, followed by a long decline. As its physical situation has become ever more precarious over recent years, the fascination it holds becomes more intense – a curious mixture of the romantic and the sinister.

Venice was the catalyst for the conception and realisation of *Host*, an installation by Pierre d'Avoine Architects in collaboration with the artists Heather Ackroyd and Dan Harvey. Pierre d'Avoine was invited by the Public Art Commissions Agency (PACA) to team up with an artist, and compete for a commission to create a piece in Venice which would coincide with the Art and Architecture Biennales planned to run simultaneously in 1995. The idea was that the piece would represent an embodiment of the dialogue between art and architecture. In the event, the Architecture Biennale was postponed until the following year, and the project with it. *Host* was shown at the Nuova Icona gallery on the Giudecca, which curated the three-week, site-specific installation in collaboration with PACA.

The resulting work read on one level as a commentary on architecture, both in the specific context of Venice, and in a broader context, transcending the particularity of place. As such, it successfully fused the interests and concerns which d'Avoine, Ackroyd and Harvey had been pursuing in their different ways before the collaboration, and which formed the common ground which made such a collaboration possible. Both parties had a strong interest in the concept of process, or growth and transformation, for which Venice provided a stimulating setting. In d'Avoine's architectural projects, there is always the sense that things are not quite what they seem to be, while Harvey and Ackroyd have made their name with a series of

installations using growing grass and crystals as the primary form-making materials.

Host consisted of three parts, in which the form of the aedicule ('little building'), or primitive hut, was the unifying factor. This form, which in the course of its history was eventually debased into a simple two-dimensional decorative device, embodies the fundamental symbolism of architecture as shelter, or 'host', and continues to be the basis of a universal architecture of the imagination. During the Classical era it became inherent to the architectural style of the time, and is clearly represented in the characteristic pedimented facades of the villas and churches designed by Palladio – the Venetian architect par eminence.

The Nuova Icona, where the gallery element of the installation was shown, is located not far from Palladio's Redentore Church. A series of white plaster aedicules, each transformed by different processes of erosion by water, elevated on metal legs, contrasted with 49 smaller mud aedicules planted close together on the floor at the end of the long main space. In the square gallery opening from this space, a much larger aedicule was suspended from the ceiling. Occupying almost the whole room, it was constructed out of sheets of altar bread embossed with the crucifix which were linked together like chain mail and hung from an open metal roof frame. Underneath was a shallow metal tray full of red wine, which reflected both the structure above, and also the room around it, capturing and holding the changing light.

These pieces explored a range of materials from the most 'base' to the most ethereal, which was emphasised by the powerful odours of mud, wine, and even plaster permeating the archetypal pure 'white' gallery space. The installation embodied at a direct physical level an idea of a process of transformation and erosion ultimately embracing the concept of transubstantiation itself in which the host is transformed into flesh during the

celebration of mass in the Roman Catholic Church. These are processes which have a special pertinence to Venice – not only physically, but also metaphorically, insofar as the city's identity has always comprised a potent mixture of splendour, sensuality, decadence and corruption, in which the Church itself historically had a large part to play. Venice's own relationship with the lagoon can be compared to that of host and parasite, and the analogy extended further to embrace architecture itself – host to mankind, yet, increasingly, a parasite on earth.

The second element of the installation was sited just across the Giudecca, in the disused chapel of San Ludovico. Once again, the space was almost entirely filled with the structure of an aedicule raised upon legs – like the stilts of Venice – transformed into a live thing, covered with grass. As the grass slowly grew to maturity, and then began to wither and die, the changes taking place in the 'little house' altered one's perception of the space within the building.

Finally, the third and most controversial element of the installation consisted of two chrome-plated condom vending machines marked 'Host' which, fixed to walls outside the two venues, brought the work right out into the street. Operated by tokens, these machines dispensed to somewhat bewildered passers-by slim packets containing three circular wafers of altar bread, all decorated with the image of the aedicule.

It was this element of the installation which embodied the most pointed reference to the Church, highlighting the ecclesiastical reference in the use of the term 'host' in perhaps an irreverent way (although it seemed to be the host aedicule in the gallery which the Venetian public found the more disturbing). However, it would be a mistake to interpret the work as being motivated simply by subversive intent; it is a piece which weaves a web of meaning at many different levels, and a thing of considerable beauty.

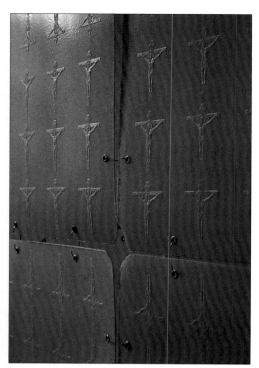

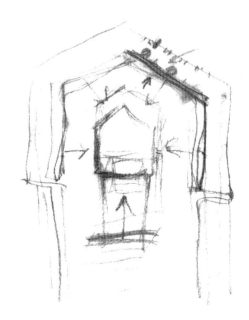

*Installation in Nuova Icona, Square Gallery –
ABOVE, L TO R: View of aedicule, altar bread,
steel, wine, from Long Gallery; aedicule;
aedicule interior;* CENTRE, L to R: Host
Machine, *Bar La Palanca, Giudecca;* Host
Machine *close up; aedicule, clay, grass seed,
black pigment, Oratorio di San Ludovico;*
LEFT: Host *concept sketch*

ABOVE: *Aedicule, clay, grass seed, black pigment, Oratorio di San Ludovico; RIGHT: Plan of installation at Nuova Icona Gallery*

RICHARD WILSON

THE JOINT IS JUMPING

Baltic Flour Mills, Gateshead

Richard Wilson's facade proposal is part of the planned conversion of the currently disused Baltic Flour Mills, Gateshead, into a new museum of contemporary art for the North East of England. The project was developed by Gateshead Council and the RIBA, who organised a national competition to find the best design concept.

Ellis Williams & Partners were awarded first prize in the competition for their proposal for an art complex incorporating work spaces, display space and educational facilities to promote contemporary art of the highest international level. Construction is planned to start in 1998 and to be completed by late 1999.

Richard Wilson was originally invited to produce a proposal for the Baltic Four Mill facade as part of 'Year of the Visual Arts 1996' in the North East. His scheme, however, was co-opted as part of the building's design and will therefore become a permanent artwork overlooking the River Tyne and the city of Newcastle.

The proposal involves outlining the geometry of the river-facing facade of the Flour Mills with neon lighting. Two neon 'outlines' will be placed; one delineating the building's edges, the other an identical linear repeat but shifted by 10 degrees from the upper right corner of the facade. The neon circuits will flick on and off, creating the impression that the building is in motion.

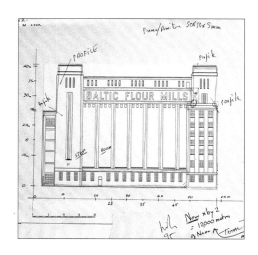

DOVECOT ARTS CENTRE
Stockton-on-Tees

In his public artwork for the new Dovecot Arts Centre in Stockton-on-Tees, England, Richard Wilson has elected to work with the imagery of the existing architecture as a means of focusing attention upon the new building and on its function as a live performance space.

During construction of the building, Wilson proposes to install a purpose-built, eight-metre-diameter 'bearing' into the facade. The portion of the facade positioned within this bearing will revolve back and forth like a 'swingboat' at approximately the same speed as the minute hand of a clock, so that its movement at any given moment is indiscernible to the passer-by.

The artwork is conceived as being individual and distinctive, yet at the same time acting as a 'flag' for the architecture, without distracting the viewer from the design of the new building. The work is also intended to announce the building's function.

The high level of integration between art and architecture is perhaps unusual for public art commissioned in this manner, and has necessitated extensive collaboration between the artist, the architects RHWL, the project structural engineers, and Price & Myers Structural Engineers, who are working specifically to realise the incorporation of the 'bearing' into the building. It is hoped that the high level of integration in this project will create a discrete yet fundamental shift in the way the architecture is perceived.

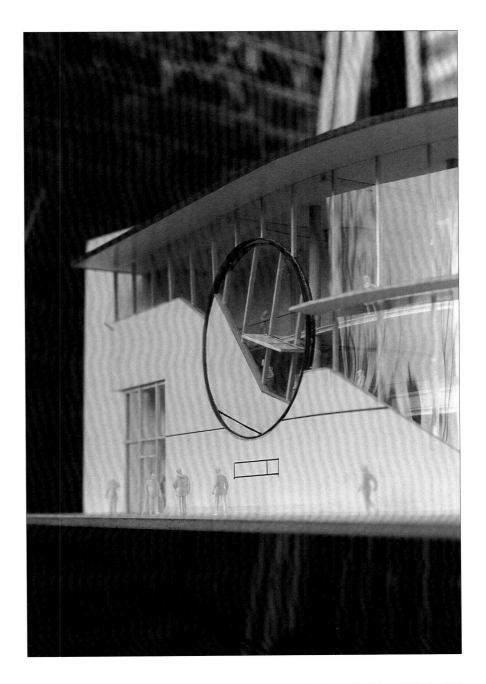

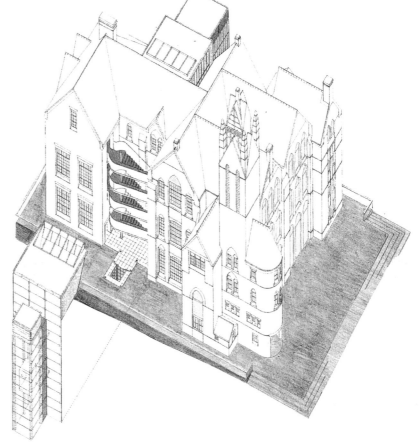

*FROM ABOVE: View of Oozells Street building;
interior work in progress; axonometric of Levitt
Bernstein proposal*

TANIA KOVATS

IN COLLABORATION WITH LEVITT BERNSTEIN ASSOCIATES
New Ikon Gallery, Birmingham

Tania Kovats' involvement with architects Levitt Bernstein as artist on the design team for the new Ikon Gallery in Oozells Street, Birmingham is unusual because whilst she acknowledged the expectation for her to produce some form of 'signature' artwork, the majority of her input has, in fact, been defined by her willingness to apply sensibility to design problems – rather than simply imposing her work on to the building.

The lack of emphasis placed upon the creation of a signature work makes Kovats' involvement quite distinct from the conventional involvement of artists in such projects. Kovats is uneasy about the notion of permanently-sited public work, and has been driven by a desire to harmonise her proposed intervention with the building, giving it a stealth-like presence within the scheme.

The proposal displays a particular sensitivity to context by demarcating the territory of the gallery from surrounding development, and placing the building on a tapered, black slate 'plinth'. The function of the plinth is to resolve the series of widely varying ground levels upon which the building sits – an example of the 'problem solving' nature of Kovats' involvement.

The intervention has the effect of framing the building as an object, but it also clearly remains a space to be animated by its users, therefore developing a dual status. Drawing on her stated desire to 'make invisible objects rather than material objects', Kovats has created an architectural intervention that is in some ways invisible – producing a 'presence' which is firmly in opposition to the conventional language of public art. She has said about the project: 'Artists and architects working together on projects or within education should not be seen as a defensive or opportunistic gesture. Schools of architecture or art are schools of culture, not schools of geniuses. In this project client, architect and artist will all have contributed to the negotiation of difficulty.'

Simon Morrissey

Interior of Oozells Street building before renovation

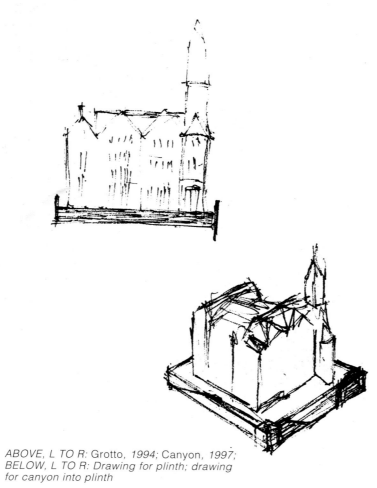

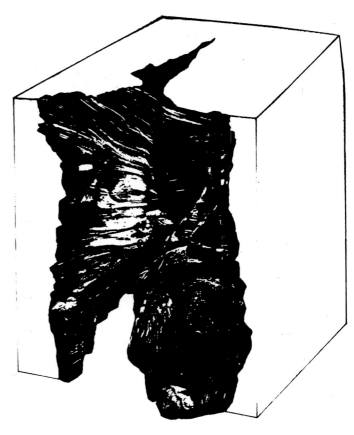

*ABOVE, L TO R: Grotto, 1994; Canyon, 1997;
BELOW, L TO R: Drawing for plinth; drawing
for canyon into plinth*